Can couples really remain passionate when they are also parents? "Yes," say the Arps. I highly recommend this wonderful collection of practical steps for keeping the spice in your marriage while living in the family lane.

—Scott M. Stanley, Ph.D.
Marital Researcher and co-author of
Fighting for Your Marriage

This book is a great resource for couples and parents! And it's delightful reading! I plan to recommend it to all the families I work with and teach.

—Martha Baldwin Beveridge, M.S.S.W., B.C.D.
Certified Imago Relationship Therapist
and President-elect of the
Association for Imago Relationship

This book does more than talk about how having kids can drain romance from marriage—it tells parents how to revive their love life. A must read!

—Bill Perkins

RESOURCES BY DAVID AND CLAUDIA ARP

Books
10 Great Dates to Revitalize Your Marriage
The Second Half of Marriage
Where the Wild Strawberries Grow
The Love Book
52 Dates for You and Your Mate
The Ultimate Marriage Builder
The Marriage Track
60 One-Minute Marriage Builders
60 One-Minute Family Builders
60 One-Minute Memory Makers

Video Curriculum
10 Great Dates to Revitalize Your Marriage
PEP Groups for MOMS
PEP Groups for PARENTS OF TEENS
MOM & DAD's Support Group

Audio Pages
The Second Half of Marriage

Books by Claudia Arp
Almost 13
Beating the Winter Blues
52 Ways to Be a Great Mother-in-Law
Sanity in the Summertime (coauthored with Linda Dillow)
The Big Book of Family Fun (coauthored with Linda Dillow)

For more information:
About **Marriage Alive Couple Enrichment Resources** contact:
Marriage Alive International, Inc., P. O. Box 31408, Knoxville,
TN 37930. Phone: (423) 691-8505 Fax: (423) 691-1575.
www.marriagealive.com.

Love Life for Parents

How to Have Kids and a Sex Life Too

David & Claudia Arp

ZondervanPublishingHouse

Grand Rapids, Michigan

A Division of HarperCollinsPublishers

Love Life for Parents
Copyright © 1998 by David and Claudia Arp

Requests for information should be addressed to:

 ZondervanPublishingHouse
Grand Rapids, Michigan 49530

Library of Congress Cataloging-in-Publication Data

Arp, David, 1940–
    Love Life for Parents: how to have kids and a sex life too / David and
Claudia Arp.
        p.   cm.
    Includes bibliographical references.
    ISBN: 0-310-20715-0 (softcover)
    1. Parents—United States—Sexual behavior. 2. Parents—United
States—Time management. 3. Sex in marriage—United States. 4.
Parenting—United States. I. Arp, Claudia. II. Title.
HQ755.8.A733   1997
646.7'8—dc21   97-39951
                                                           CIP

Published in association with the literary agency of Alive Communications,
1465 Kelly Johnson Blvd., Suite 320, Colorado Springs, CO 80920

Interior design by Sherri L. Hoffman

Printed in the United States of America

---

98 99 00 01 02 /❖ DC/ 10 9 8 7 6 5 4 3 2 1

*To all husbands and wives who, in the middle of
the active parenting years, are seeking to find the time
and energy to love each other*

Contents

~

Acknowledgments

We gratefully acknowledge the contributions of the following people:

— All the couples who have participated in our parenting and Marriage Alive seminars over the years and who have shared with us your stuggles and success stories;

— All those who responded to our Love, Sex, Marriage, and Kids survey. Your input was invaluable!

— The Geisters, who so generously loaned us their lovely vacation home in Germany's Black Forest for us to write the initial draft of this book. Thank you!

— The reseachers and authors we quoted, for your sound work, which gives a solid base for the cause of marriage education;

— Our publisher, Scott Bolinder, for your friendship and for giving us this opportunity to help parents also be lovers;

— Our editor, Sandy Vander Zicht for your expertise and nudge toward excellence;

— Our development editor, Mary McNeil, for your helpful suggestions that make this book practical and fun;

— Jody Langley for making this book look so inviting;

— Our "in-house" team—Laurie Clark, and Jonathan and Autumn Whiteman Arp for your encouragement and help along the way.

— Our literary agent, Greg Johnson of Alive Communications, for being our advocate.

One

~

When Lovers
Become Parents

Camping! I hate it!" Claudia said, tears welling up in her eyes. Equally frustrated, Dave stared at her in silence. Lying in our makeshift bed in our white Volkswagen camper, we listened to the beating of the rain on the cold metal roof. The raindrops drummed the same boring cadence, drop after drop—not unlike our ho-hum love life.

But this evening should have been different. We had plans. Earlier that day, we had marched our three sons—ages six, four, and fifteen months—all over London, doing everything from watching the changing of the guard at Buckingham Palace to climbing the Tower Bridge. We wore them out. We knew that after they were snug in their sleeping bags, the night would be ours. Following our game plan, all the boys were settled and sleeping soundly in the adjoining tent—or so we thought. Then a familiar cry pierced the darkness. Another ear infection! Why did this feel so familiar?

Finally the boys were back to sleep, but the episode had destroyed any desire for romance in their parents—well, at least in one of the parents—which added to the existing tension in our relationship.

The previous month we had moved our family of five to Europe. Stressful. Exhausting. The move had taken its toll on our love life. After searching for weeks for a place to rent, the house we finally found was not available for two more weeks. The solution? A family vacation! So we packed our Volkswagen camper and headed for London. With a tent plus our camper, surely we could find some privacy. What a myth!

Now here we were in London—one big happy family. Physically we were in each other's faces as we lay in our camper that humid, rainy night. Emotionally we were on opposite sides of a canyon we didn't know how to bridge. We felt isolated, misunderstood, alone.

"You're the one who suggested that we camp in London," Dave said.

"I know," Claudia snapped, "but camping with three boys isn't the fun camping was before we became parents. I wish we were alone. I wish—"

Our conversation was abruptly interrupted by another shrill cry. "Not again," Claudia moaned as she got up to rescue our toddler son. Pulling at his ear, he clung to Claudia, absolutely refusing to go back to his makeshift playpen crib in the tent. Our love life was on hold for yet another night.

WHEN BABY MAKES THREE

Never did we dream how much children would affect our relationship and our love life. We had been married for almost four years when the three simple words, "It's a boy!" changed our lives forever. Six pounds and seven ounces of dynamite invaded our lives. Actually, the arrival of our first child felt as if someone rolled a hand grenade under our bed. It blew away our sex life and caused mass confusion! While adjusting to thoughts of parenthood and preparing for the actual birth experience had been all-consuming, we had both looked forward to rediscovering sexual intimacy—but neither of us realized the difficulties that lay ahead.

As new parents, we were overwhelmed, exhausted, and insecure. We kept waiting for life to return to normal. It never did. When Claudia went back for her six-week postpartum checkup, the doctor told her we could resume sex as usual. Who was he kidding? After the birth of each of our sons, it was several months before sex was even comfortable for Claudia, much less enjoyable. And it was a rare occasion indeed when we weren't too tired to even attempt sex. The standard pain associated with delivering an almost-seven-pound bundle of energy and nursing a ravenous baby several hours a day left Claudia exhausted and wanting sleep, not sex. Dave quickly learned how to change diapers and became the master middle-of-the-night rocker and walker, which left him uncharacteristically grumpy in the mornings. Our easygoing, relaxed routine was history.

Add two more kids, and life began to spin out of control. We had almost given up on both sleep and sex at that point. Plus, our sexual desires for each other were out of sync. Claudia would crawl in bed after the late-night feeding of son number three with Dave, the night owl, ready for the loving to begin! Fat chance! We also remember those early mornings when Claudia, the morning lark, woke up in an amorous mood but couldn't shake Dave awake. He had walked the floor until 4:00 A.M. with our newest bundle of joy. We began to wonder if this were "natural" birth control. At that point we would have gladly traded our sex life for the rare pleasure of eight hours of uninterrupted sleep!

WHAT'S COUPLE TIME?

*W*hat happened to our relaxed and enjoyable "times for two"? We forgot what it was like to have uninterrupted time to talk, love, and dream together. Everyday intimacy, so familiar before our sons joined our family, was now missing. Although we loved our sons and loved being parents, we missed the easygoing communication that filled the first years of our marriage.

The same scenario is played out time and time again as partners become parents. Our friend Julie exclaimed, "You were right. You tried to tell me what it would be like after our son, Jason, was born. You told me that I would be frazzled and exhausted, that Frank and I would have to fight for time alone, and that we would even ignore our dog. I just didn't believe you! But exhaustion is just one part of parenthood.

"Before becoming a parent, I really thought I could have it all," Julie continued, "—marriage, motherhood, a fulfilling career, and a love life—but now I wonder what happened. Besides always being tired, after breast-feeding Jason or changing his dirty diaper, I'm just not that interested in sex."

Another complication when baby makes three is the difficulty many couples have leaving their baby. Dating and nights out become vague memories. You become so child-focused that your marriage and your sex life are placed on the back burner to simmer and then boil over as unattended conflicts and frustrations arise.

Not only is there no time for dating but what happened to romance? Leisurely times for romancing each other, for cuddling, and for feeling cherished and loved are no longer available. Besides, you're too tired to even remember what your love life was like before children.

But becoming parents should not make us celibate! How can parents find time for sex *and* romance? We never found time; we had to *make* time! And that's what we want to share with you in the following chapters. Based on our experience of parenting three active boys, our work with couples in our Marriage Alive seminars over the past two decades, and the input from hundreds of parents from our national Love, Marriage, Sex, and Kids survey, we want to share some secrets we discovered for having kids and a love life too!

GREAT SEX

*Y*es, you can have great sex. When we talk about sex, we're talking about much more than sexual intercourse; we're talking about developing and nurturing a love life. Having kids and a love life is much more than carving out ten minutes for physical release. "You have to take time to talk and listen to each other," said one mom. "I want time for intimacy—for leisurely back rubs and cups of tea before making love. You can't do that in ten minutes after the news."

A fulfilling love life is multidimensional—especially for the mom! Her desire for tenderness, for feeling loved, cherished, and romanced, is as important as the dad's desire for passion, excitement, and quick release. Great sex involves passion, excitement, tenderness, and romance.

The vital love life you may have had before kids may now be in a low-maintenance survival mode. And if your love life wasn't so great to begin with, by now you may have given up all hope. Adding a child influences nearly every aspect of your relationship. The good news is that with the right attitude and commitment, the impact can be thoroughly positive.

While our lives were changed forever after kids arrived, in time we weren't quite as exhausted, and with stubborn determination we found ways to stay connected. Eventually our sex life rebounded. But it did not happen overnight or even in a few months. Just how long your own journey back to a healthy sex life will take depends on many factors: the type and difficulty of birth, the temperament of the child and the parents, the amount of support you get from family and others, and of course, your job situation.

Our initial rebound was followed by years of working at having and maintaining an intentional love life. Life will never be quite the same again, but you *can* have kids and a love life too.

YOU CAN BUILD A CREATIVE LOVE LIFE

We had just begun the session in our Marriage Alive seminar entitled "Building a Creative Love Life" when a young mom asked in sheer frustration, "What love life? I don't even have a *life*—much less a *love* life! For me life is too complex—the children, our own parents, jobs, church, the yard—I feel like I'm stuck in the fast lane with no way to slow down. Love life? I'd just like to have two hours alone!"

We were happy to tell our seminar participant—and you as well—that there is hope! You can overcome the barriers to creating a high-priority love life in the midst of parenting pressures. In the coming chapters we'll help you evaluate your parenting and marriage perspectives. Where does your marriage relationship really fit into your life? To have time for sex, your marriage doesn't have to compete with your children for time, but it should still be the primary relationship in your life.

Feeling Overwhelmed? Take This Quiz!

True or False

Give yourself one point for each false answer.

_____ Your ultimate sexual fantasy is eight hours of uninterrupted sleep.

_____ Getting "turned on" means the baby's monitor is set.

You're celebrating your anniversary at a great restaurant.

_____ While waiting for the appetizer, you fall asleep.

_____ During the main course, you cut your partner's meat.

_____ As you're ordering dessert, you check to make sure your spouse has cleaned his or her plate.

_____ Back at home, your partner approaches you with loving caresses—that's the last thing you can remember. ZZZZZZZZZ!

Scoring

6   Wow! How did you do it? We're impressed with your success!

4–5   You're on the right track—not completely overwhelmed.

0–3   You *are* overwhelmed!

Whatever your score, if you are a parent, you will probably at times feel overwhelmed. So when you feel completely overwhelmed by your circumstances, take a deep breath and remember a time when you felt *most* competent and capable. Perhaps it was completing a project at work, or maybe it was successfully pulling off your first dinner party, or it was back when you ran a student organization in college or when you built a float for your high school homecoming parade. Now tell yourself that *you can feel that good* about parenting and your love life too. You need only harness the energy, enthusiasm, and creativity that you applied to that previous situation and use it now to build the life you want.

How Children Can Enrich Your Love Life

- *Children remind you that you are one.* Each time you see Junior's toes, you have to admit they are just like Dad's, or Susie's sweet grin is a picture of Mom's smile that won you over years ago and still melts your heart. Children remind you they are here because you love each other.

- *Children encourage creativity.* Since children present many obstacles to finding time alone together, you must discover creative ways of getting together. And the very essence of romance thrives on obstacles, delays, separation, and dreams. Think back to before you married and how you worked so hard to be together! Now do it again!

- *Children promote appreciation.* Because it's more challenging to make time for sex, you appreciate it more when you love each other.

- *Children encourage maturity.* You are now the parent! Now is the time to be the best person you can be. Children will mimic your behavior—good or bad. So take this opportunity to make some improvements in broad areas of your life—self-discipline, exercise, internal reflection, spiritual disciplines—to be a better model for your children. Don't be too hard on yourself and don't expect too much too soon. But do make a conscious effort every day to be your absolute best.

We will consider how a great sex life is the result of building a healthy marriage and a healthy lifestyle. Then we will identify the basic building blocks of any healthy relationship: positive communication, encouragement, shared core beliefs, and commitment to growth.

Understanding your own expectations and those of your spouse will help you be more understanding and more sexually responsive. Then we will tackle the two biggest barriers to loving your partner while parenting your kids— lack of time and lack of energy. And what about those lovely little products of your family planning? You must teach your children to respect your marriage and your need for time alone.

Learning to have fun together while parenting your children is an essential component to a healthy marriage now and for your lifetime together. To that end we will give you some tips for planning getaways and finding daily "mini-moments" for loving. And then we will help you come up with your own strategy for loving each other for a lifetime.

We realize that if you are like most parents who read this book, you will probably be interrupted in the next five minutes, so sprinkled throughout the book are our best quick tips for enhancing your love life, as well as tips from those parents who participated in our survey. Feel free to graze in this book for a sixty-second snack or for a leisurely hour of feasting. Now is the time to *make* time to build a love life that will remain vital when the children leave home. Remember, your children will wait while you build your love life, but your love life won't wait until your children grow up. Now is the time to make time for sex!

Two

What's a Love Life?

*T*ake a trip with us. Think back to those magic moments when you discovered your love for each other. Do you remember the chemistry? The tingle when you held hands? That first kiss? The intense desire to be intimate with each other? The overwhelming need to be with the one you love?

At the beginning of our relationship, Dave was in college at Georgia Tech in Atlanta, and Claudia was at the University of Georgia in Athens. Our thoughts were consumed with each other and with scheming how we could get together. And our private times together were simple. Sure, we had long conversations, but the icing on the cake was the cuddles, kisses, hand-holding, and hugs. We didn't need to evaluate or discuss our expectations or disappointments, because everything was so simple! We understood what then was the essential component of a love life—just being together!

Then we got married and things changed. No longer did we have to scheme how to get together. The essential component of our love life was no longer defined by simply being together. We, like most couples, entered marriage with different backgrounds, attitudes, and baggage to unpack and process. Also, we understood little about gender differences and our different biological and psychological drives. All of these factors complicated our love life.

The intense desire for romance and to be together before marriage was replaced by a more complicated set of needs and desires—to be understood, to be recognized, and to be respected as individuals. Emotional contact was just as important as physical contact.

A healthy love life blends both the emotional and physical sides of love and is like a diamond with many facets. Just which facets gleam at any given moment depends on how you are looking at the diamond and upon the type of light enhancing the diamond. While the intense physical desire for sex is one facet, many other facets—intimacy, romance, playfulness, communication, thoughtfulness, laughter, and so on—add even greater depth and beauty to a love relationship.

THE BEST FACETS OF A HEALTHY AND SATISFYING LOVE LIFE

From our survey we learned what couples considered to be the best aspects of their love life, and how successful couples manage to have kids and a love life too. While the responses varied, several themes emerged as essential components for a truly healthy love life: trust, mutuality, honesty, intimacy, pleasure, and sex. We want to give you a picture of what an ideal love life might look like. It is our hope that by laying the framework for a star-studded love life, you will be able to pinpoint areas in your own love life that need fine-tuning. Then you can work toward your own ideal.

Trust—Feeling Safe with Each Other

A basic component of any friendship, trust is essential in a romantic relationship and is foundational for all that is to come. You must trust that you are safe with your partner, that your partner will not harm you or betray you, and that you can share your most prized possession—yourself— with your partner.

Realistically, in a relationship that is as close as marriage is, from time to time you will let each other down. Maybe you're shouldering most of the parenting responsibilities. Your mate keeps promising to help, but it just doesn't happen. You feel overloaded but your mate doesn't want to discuss it. Or perhaps at a recent dinner party, your spouse inadvertently commented on the extra ten pounds you can't seem to lose. Or maybe your spouse never seems to make good on a promise to go away for a weekend together without the kids. While these may not qualify as huge betrayals, they can hurt the "trust factor" if they are habitual, not just occasional, occurrences.

The next time trust is broken, talk about it. Tell your partner how you feel: "Last night when you fell asleep in the middle of the video, I was disappointed. Before dinner I thought you were sending out signals that you wanted to make love—then you went to sleep." Talking about your frustrations and feelings will help your partner know you want to work at finding solutions. Just talking openly will build trust. (Communication tips in chapter 4 will help you open up and talk

Couples' Responses to the Question, What Are the Best Aspects of Your Love Life?

- Intimacy, openness, and honesty
- Being soul mates
- Pleasing each other
- Determination
- Great sex life
- Romantic rituals
- Tenderness and touching
- Fun times together
- Warmth and sensitivity
- Trusting each other

about intimate subjects.) Brainstorm together and suggest ways you can avoid trust busters in the future. Perhaps your spouse needs a reminder when he or she is about to break trust. Maybe your expectations are too high—for instance, at the Arps', if we're both tired and then turn on the TV or plug in a video, one of us will be sound asleep before love-making can begin, even if we're anticipating having sex!

If for some reason there has been a serious breach of trust such as lying, deception, or an emotional affair with a coworker—you need to rebuild trust before you can work on the other aspects of your love relationship. Don't be afraid to enlist the assistance of a professional counselor or pastor. Sometimes the best gift you can give to your marriage is getting some short-term professional help. Trust can be rebuilt in a broken relationship, but it will take work and commitment on the part of both partners.

Seek constantly to build and affirm the trust that exists between you and your spouse. Easily taken for granted when present, and devastating when absent, the bond of trust is fundamental to intimacy.

Trust Builders

- Saying you are going to take the trash out—and actually doing it!
- Helping out when your partner is on overload
- Giving your mate an honest compliment
- Apologizing when you are wrong
- Accepting your spouse's apology without saying, "I told you so"
- Taking a nap together
- Keeping your humor when the wee ones have exhausted you

Mutuality—Freely Choosing to Love Each Other

Each partner must want to be in the relationship. Having a mutual relationship involves a decision to choose each other above all others and to make your relationship a priority—to be willing to grow together and to adapt to each other's changing needs over the years. We realize there are times when you would like to take a hike or just have some time alone, but in a mutual relationship, partners generally like to be together—even with the normal ups and downs all relationships experience.

We all know what it feels like when someone we are with doesn't want to be with us. Perhaps it was when you had a blind date in college or when you dragged your spouse along to one of your favorite activities and sensed your partner's resentment. We remember one such occasion.

After getting a sitter for our two preschoolers, Claudia dragged Dave to a lecture about the secrets of a successful marriage. The presentation left Dave—who was there under duress—cold. It wasn't that Dave didn't want to be with Claudia. He didn't want to be at the lecture and felt Claudia had manipulated and coerced him into going. Well, he was right; she had. In retrospect, if Claudia had been less insistent, we probably could have found an activity that would have

> ### Affirming the Bond of Trust
>
> Make a list of reasons why you trust your spouse, using your spouse's name as an acrostic. For each letter give a character quality that promotes trust. For instance, I wrote, "I trust you because you
>
> D— dare to always be truthful;
>
> A— affirm your absolute loyalty to our marriage;
>
> V— value our relationship above all others;
>
> E— energize our relationship with fun and laughter."
>
> Claudia

Something to Ponder

Women are usually more comfortable sharing details of their lives and relationship difficulties with their close female friends, while most men would never even broach these subjects with their male friends. Some men would be hurt if they knew what was said over phone lines and cups of tea. They may even consider it a breach of trust or an act of disloyalty. Even though he is not there to hear you, keep your husband's feelings in mind as you think about divulging personal matters to your friends.

Dave

---

pleased us both—like going out for dinner or coffee. Now that would have fostered mutuality.

Power plays and manipulation destroy the potential for mutuality and love. When one partner always wants his or her own way and resorts to nagging, threatening, or manipulating to get it, the relationship is sabotaged. Unloving actions such as these can even cause the other to question not only the relationship but also his or her own sense of personal worth and identity.

Think about how good it feels when your spouse lets you know he or she wants to be with you, through a twinkle in the eye, a gentle caress of the hand, or a loving comment. This quiet understanding naturally breeds security, confidence, and romance and diminishes the importance of the little irritations and repeated arguments that often sabotage relationships.

But don't just assume your mate knows that you are glad to be married to him or her. Regularly find verbal and nonverbal ways to let him or her know! You'll be pleased at how this little habit makes both of you feel more confident and secure in your relationship.

Honesty—Openly Communicating Your True Feelings

Honesty is as necessary to a healthy relationship as sunlight is to flowers and trees. If spouses do not have the ability to relate their needs and desires truthfully and without manipulation, their marriage cannot grow. This is an acquired skill. As parents, you have likely developed the ability to talk openly and honestly with each other about some things—bedtime routines, how you will approach potty training or discipline. But to apply this frankness to intimate subjects takes vulnerability, commitment, and practice. However, the rewards of being open and honest are great. King Solomon of ancient days summed it up well: "An honest answer is like a kiss on the lips."[1] (Chapter 4 will give you tips for communicating openly and honestly— especially about your love life.)

"Mutually Devoted to You!"

Ways to demonstrate your devotion to your partner:

- Present your mate with a long-stemmed rose.
- Create your own greeting card and indicate it is from "one who married the very best!"
- Frame a picture of the two of you.
- Write a love note on the steamed bathroom mirror.
- Say, "Go for it. I know you can do it!"
- Send a love e-mail or fax.
- Hug for ten seconds.
- Give your spouse a sincere compliment in the company of his or her friends.
- Take a hike—together!

Bad Habits Are for Breaking!

Spend some time really listening to how you and your mate communicate. Are there some negative patterns (taunting, nagging, dominating) that might be barriers to more intimate and vulnerable communication? Perhaps you have the tendency to repeat your request to the point of nagging. "You forgot to buckle your seat belt" can be said in different ways, many of them considered nagging. Try using just one or two words: "Seat belt!" That may be more effective than five nagging statements—and ultimately safer.

Make a mental note of your bad habits (or write them down and keep them in your wallet, if you need to) and try to eliminate them from your conversations. A greater civility and the potential for true intimacy will result.

Intimacy—Being Soul Mates and Feeling Close

Based on trust, freely entered into by both partners, and fueled by honesty, intimacy is the intangible quality of unity, understanding, and synergy that can move a relationship from acquaintance or friend to lover and soul mate. And like all of the previously mentioned components of a healthy love life, intimacy ebbs and flows over the life of a marriage.

Parenting can challenge marital intimacy. "Before kids our lovemaking used to be great," writes one mom. "Now I'm too tired with caregiving, keeping everything on track at home, and managing a part-time job. I'm just so dormant. Is this normal? My husband is still interested, but I'm not. To be honest, I don't really want to find time for sex."

If intimacy is low in a relationship, partners are not motivated to communicate on anything more than a superficial level, physical contact is perfunctory if not completely absent, and marital satisfaction and joy are lacking.

On the other hand, couples who experience high intimacy often laugh a little more and a little louder, enjoy touching and being touched, are more likely to feel understood and accepted, and are generally more secure in all aspects of their life.

Maintaining a basic level of intimacy encourages the sharing of dreams, needs, fears, and desires. Staying intimate requires time and effort, but it's vital to a good marriage.

Pleasure—Giving Joy and Comfort to Each Other

Not the sole purpose of a marriage but certainly an important part of any loving relationship, pleasure takes many forms. The comforting cup of coffee regularly shared over the Saturday paper, the hearty laugh shared over a joke, the much-needed one-minute shoulder rub, the spontaneous cuddles, hugs, and kisses—all of these are pleasurable experiences and necessary for a vibrant love life. But many times the tedium of everyday life creeps in and fills the spaces that should be saved for laughter, fun, and pleasure.

Many of the daily frustrations are magnified when we have children. Constant tiredness, continual interruptions in our already overcrowded days, attempts to see through the smoke screen of misunderstanding, lack of time to talk and resolve issues, and lack of privacy and time together

Intimacy in a Nutshell

Intimacy is the desire to know and be known deeply by the other.

Think about these two questions:

1. What are some of the ways I would like to know my spouse more intimately?

2. What are some of the ways I would like my spouse to know me more intimately?

Discovering the Joy of Intentional Pleasure

Giving and receiving pleasure doesn't always come naturally. Don't be discouraged if it's been a while since you've enjoyed an intimate, romantic rendezvous with your mate. Give yourself a break. You can get back into the habit. The mastery of any skill takes practice! So take the time today to plan a "pleasure time for two." If you have a home with an oversized bathroom, meet there after the kids are in bed!

are just a few of the frustrations parents face daily. Pleasure? What's that? But when a relationship loses its spark and joy, it loses much of its purpose and grounding, too often leaving spouses wondering why they are in the relationship in the first place. While we love and enjoy our children, we must not let them become our primary source of happiness. We must recapture the vision for our own intimate pleasure.

Giving each other pleasure and having fun together should be the most natural thing in the world—but it isn't. It takes work. You must be intentional, so pull out your calendar and plan romantic moments as well as fun times together.

If you are short on ideas, don't worry. To get you started, we've included many ideas throughout this book. And after you practice the fine art of pleasure and fun for a while, your own creativity will flourish.

Sex—Joining Together Physically and Loving Each Other

The culmination of a great love life *is* sex. Intended for more than procreation, an intimate, pleasurable sexual experience is the most intense and intimate thing a couple can share. In their book *The Good Marriage*, Judith Wallerstein

Intended for Pleasure!

Rebuilding your sex life is not a selfish physical desire; it is a necessary step toward growing and solidifying your marriage for a lifetime. Sex is intended for procreation, but it is also intended for pleasure. Sex expresses love between husband and wife. Thousands of years ago Solomon, a writer of proverbs, encouraged spouses to indulge in sexual pleasure by offering this blessing: "May your fountain be blessed, and may you rejoice in the wife of your youth. A loving doe, a graceful deer—may her breasts satisfy you always, may you ever be captivated by her love."[2] That sounds erotic to us. King Solomon's wonderful love story is found in Song of Songs. You may even want to read these love poems out loud together.

and Sandra Blakeslee emphasize the importance of sex: "It is very important for all couples to find ways to protect their privacy, to cherish their sexual relationship, and to guard it fiercely. A richly rewarding and stable sex life is not just a fringe benefit, it is the central task of marriage. In a good marriage, sex and love are inseparable. Sex serves a very serious function in maintaining both the quality and stability of the relationship, replenishing emotional reserves, and strengthening the marital bond."[3]

Realizing how important a good sex life is to a good marriage, you need to make time for rebuilding your sex life.

HAVING A FIVE-STAR LOVE LIFE

Understanding the components of love—trust, mutuality, honesty, intimacy, pleasure, and sex—will help you create your own diamond-studded love life. Far from being a marital add-on, a healthy, creative love life is a key to a healthy marriage.

As you make your love life a priority, your children will not suffer! In fact, an intimate love relationship between you and your spouse will positively influence your children's future relationships.

In the next chapter you will discover ways your marriage can enrich and influence your children's lives as you put everything in its proper place. Giving yourself permission to prioritize your marriage will put you on the path to building a creative, healthy love life. Then you *can* have kids and a love life.

Are You a Five-Star Lover?

A five-star lover puts his or her partner first and seeks to give physical and emotional pleasure through a creative love life that includes

- cherishing
- romancing
- sacrificing
- caring
- respecting
- admiring

Three

~

Revive Us Again

Jan and Steve spent weeks planning their anniversary dinner. Dressed to the hilt—Jan wearing the midnight blue pantsuit their daughter, Hannah, picked out for her, and Steve in a business suit and tie chosen by their son, Max—they now sat at an elegant table for two in the most popular new restaurant in town.

Over appetizers Steve commented, "Can you believe it? We're actually away from the kids!"

Jan responded, "But it wasn't easy! I felt like an air traffic controller getting everyone's schedule to work." She rattled off how she had coordinated meals, homework, soccer practice, an alternate ballet lesson pickup, and had even found another dad to sub for Steve as a Boy Scout leader for the evening.

"Now that you brought up scouting," Steve said as their entrées arrived, "I'm concerned about the new scoutmaster and the lack of parental involvement in the troop. I just don't think the boys had adequate supervision on that last hike."

Jan had similar concerns about Hannah's kindergarten class. "But at least we have time to talk without interruption," Steve added.

Over dessert the conversation finally moved away from the kids and on to planning the family's summer vacation.

Money was tight this year, so they would have to watch every discretionary penny in order to go to the beach.

"As a matter of fact," Jan said as she sipped her after-dinner coffee, "we really ought to think about heading home. At five dollars an hour for the baby-sitter, this evening is getting expensive!"

At home, after putting the kids to bed—the baby-sitter couldn't get them to sleep on her own—Jan and Steve snuggled on the couch, all ready to watch the movie Jan had rented. She had actually found the movie they saw on their first date. It sparked romance back then. But soon, after just fifteen minutes of the movie, Jan and Steve were sleeping soundly on their very comfy and very spacious sofa.

Have you had a similar experience? Although it may have seemed like a perfectly pleasant evening, something was missing. On an evening designed to get away from kids and celebrate their marriage, Jan and Steve spent the entire time talking about their kids and their kids' activities. And when they finally did make it to what was supposed to be the romantic portion of the evening, they collapsed onto the sofa and promptly fell asleep!

You may be thinking, "Well, that's just what our lives are like now. Our world revolves around our kids, and hey, we're not ashamed of that. We love our kids and want to give them our best!" Giving your kids your best is an admirable goal. However, it does not mean giving them every thought, every minute, every conversation, and every deed.

Balancing roles as partners and parents is one of the most difficult tasks any couple can face. Start by giving yourself permission to focus on the marriage relationship. Dr. Paul Pearsall, in his book *Super Marital Sex,* writes, "As many marriages fail because of children as children fail because of faulty marriages. Until we learn that children are not special, but equal in importance to all of us, until we learn that we must not lead our lives and marriages for children but with them, we sacrifice our marriages and our own development."[1]

"BUT I FEEL GUILTY!"

*T*hat sounds great," one seminar participant said. "But I feel guilty when I don't put my children first. If I'm making my husband my priority, I'm letting other things—like my parenting role—slip."

"Feeling guilty," we told her, "is a universal experience—but is one we can overcome."

From time to time we all experience guilt, but Ellen Kreidman, in her book *Is There Sex After Kids?* says mothers experience guilt much more frequently and intensely than fathers. She writes, "Guilt is an inherited disease, one passed down from mother to daughter, generation after generation. I have found that women, especially mothers, feel guilty no matter what they do. If they stay home and bake cookies, they feel guilty because they aren't 'fulfilling' themselves with a challenging career or contributing to the family coffers. If they work full-time, they feel guilty because they aren't fully involved with their children.... And working part-time is sometimes the greatest guilt inducer of all—leaving a mother feeling bad for giving only half an effort to the kids and half an effort to her job."[2]

Today the majority of mothers work outside the home; they have less time for the rest of life, specifically their home. Whether we admit it or not, the major responsibilities in the home usually fall on the mother. With what amounts to two full-time jobs, a mother can easily feel overwhelmed and guilty. Contributing to the guilt are her high expectations, often left over from her own mother, who most likely did not work outside the home.

"In my home growing up," one mom said, "my mom was a great homemaker. You could eat off the floor. You can eat off the floor in my house, too—Cherrios, Spaghettios, Teddy Grahams, and animal crackers!"

You can't do everything. Something has to fall through the cracks. Together, you and your partner should decide what that should be. For the sake of your marriage, let it be something other than your love life. It's easy to be so child focused that you forget to focus on your partner and your own personal needs. And where does that leave your love life? One parent answered, "What love life?"

OUR PRESCRIPTION FOR A HEALTHY LOVE LIFE

To revive your love life, we suggest three steps: (1) take care of yourself; (2) be good to your marriage; (3) let your marriage be good to your children.

Take Care of Yourself

For us, nothing zaps our love life like our backs! Gone are the days when we could abuse our backs without painful consequences. Now our backs are our "pacers"—they signal when we need to slow down and take care of ourselves.

What is your pacer? Stress and tension seem to seek out the weakest part of the anatomy. Maybe your back is healthy, but you get chronic sinusitis, allergies, or migraine headaches. If we are going to make our marriage a priority and be the parents we want to be, we first need to learn to pace ourselves. So without guilt, consider ways you could be good to yourself. In chapter 8 we'll look closer at this topic.

Fourteen Ways to Take Care of Me

1. Take fifteen minutes each day to sit, read, reflect, or do whatever you want to do.
2. Get eight hours of sleep—even if you have to catch a nap before dinner or on your lunch hour.
3. Hire a baby-sitter and do whatever you want to do for a couple of hours.
4. Take a long, relaxing bath after you put the kids in bed.
5. Sit down and enjoy a cup of tea.
6. Take a short walk.
7. Exercise for fifteen minutes.
8. Watch your favorite video.
9. Browse in a bookstore.
10. Read a few pages in your favorite book.
11. Give yourself a manicure.
12. Get your hair cut.
13. Call a friend and visit for fifteen minutes.
14. Buy your favorite candy bar.

Be Good to Your Marriage

Taking time for yourself will energize you to take time for your marriage. Remember, parenting is a temporary job. Each kid will be out of your house in about eighteen years! But your mate is there for life! What can you do now to make your marriage a high priority?

Prioritizing your marriage is making your partnership with your spouse the key relationship in your home. The children will require more time, but in healthy families the marriage relationship comes first!

"When I walk in the door," one survey participant wrote, "the first thing I do is hug my spouse. The kids are next, but I think it is healthy for our children to see in practical ways how we put our love first."

Ten Ways to Be Good to Your Marriage

1. Tell your honey five reasons why you love him or her!
2. Scratch your lover's back.
3. Get up with the baby and let your spouse sleep.
4. Let voice mail collect your calls, or turn the phone ringer off.
5. Put on your spouse's favorite music.
6. Light a scented candle.
7. Eat a bowl of ice cream together after the kids are in bed.
8. Write a letter and tell your mate why you would marry him or her all over again.
9. Put sticky notes everywhere with personal messages.
10. Continue with this list until your spouse is number one in your thoughts!

Another parent told us, "I may spend hours supervising homework assignments and carting kids here and there, but each evening our children know that for fifteen minutes we are not available to them—that's our time to focus on each other. The children are to interrupt us only if the house is on fire!"

Children demand a large part of your time, and you must also devote a significant chunk of time to earning a living. Though little time may be left over, most people have some discretionary time. And discretionary time is just that—you can choose how you want to invest it.

Wise couples choose to invest some of their discretionary time in making their marriage a priority. Even if you only have a few minutes, you can invest them in your marriage. In chapter 7 we'll look closer at the time issue and help you free up minutes you didn't know you had.

Let Your Marriage Be Good to Your Children

Your marriage can influence your children in a very positive way! When children grow up in happy, intact, functional families with parents who love each other, they unconsciously learn the roles they will later need in marriage and parenthood. Actually, as you focus on your marriage, you mentor your children.

Consider three ways your marriage can benefit your children:

1. *Your Marriage Provides Stability*

A strong marriage significantly enhances children's security and stability by letting them know that the unconditional, lifelong love modeled between parents also applies to them. Even parents arguing and then making up demonstrates that life goes on and love is not diminished in the face of disagreements and stress.

"We don't try to hide our disagreements from our children," Francis, a seminar participant, told us. "They need to know that we can disagree, but we still love each other and are totally committed to our marriage and family. In my home I never heard my parents disagree. Then when I was thirteen, one day my dad just left—I didn't know anything was amiss. It was devastating!

> **Five Ways Your Marriage Can Be Good to Your Children**
>
> 1. Let your kids help you plan a surprise for their mom or dad.
> 2. Have a family hug.
> 3. Tell your child ten reasons why you love their mom or dad.
> 4. Get your kids to help you plan a date with their mom or dad.
> 5. Talk with your children about what they want in a future mate.

As a Person Thinks in Her Heart

Even now my attitude has everything to do with my contribution to our love life. But I remember when our boys were young and I was totally zapped of energy and had little desire for sex. I knew how important our sex life was to Dave, but I was only able to take the initiative to change as I worked on my attitude. I'm a thinker and as the old proverb goes, "as [a man] thinks in his heart, so is he."[3] Actually, our love life was important to me too—it's just that I was so tired, I didn't know it. For me tiredness masked desire. But when I took the time to affirm my attitude—to think with my heart—I became more interested in loving Dave, even in my exhausted state. If I started with the attitude of wanting to meet Dave's needs, most of the time my own interest was aroused!

Claudia

Life just isn't like that. My husband, Lewis, says if we agreed on everything, life would be boring. So one way we mentor our children is modeling positive ways to resolve conflict. But we also laugh and have fun together as a couple and as a family."

2. *Your Marriage Sets the Tone*

The way you relate to each other sets the atmosphere in your home. If you habitually joke and laugh together, like Francis and Lewis, your home will be a fun place to be, and your children will learn how to laugh and enjoy life. Conversely, if your kids only see you argue, they are more likely to argue. They assume arguing is just the way people interact with each other. Obviously, a healthy balance includes both confrontation and laughter.

When our children were young, Claudia was the resident worrier, while Dave was the family jokester. Together over the years we learned how to find balance—there are times for joking but also times for serious concern and conversations. But joking or serious, we tried to be real and have no hidden undertones. Nothing is worse than a home in which words are polite but underneath is hostility, bitterness, and tension.

What is the general tone of your home? Think about how you relate to each other. There is a huge chance that the way your children treat their spouses will look a lot like the way you

> Family wellness is characterized by maturity in which parental roles model the following:
>
> - How to be a man or woman
> - How to be a husband or wife
> - How to be a father or mother
> - How to achieve intimate relationships with others
> - How to be a functional, contributing human being[4]

A Lifelong Learner

My thirst for knowledge motivates me to keep making our love life a high priority. Actually, it's a key to our sexual relationship. I'm a learner and I'm still learning about Claudia and how to pleasure her. When we were first married, I realized that we both had a lot to learn and that I could take the lead in scouring resources for building a creative love life. I'm also more the explorer and experimenter, and with my gathered information Claudia was more willing to participate.

This benefited us greatly after the children started arriving: She was too exhausted to be creative, and I *always* have some energy left for sex. Claudia called it my "Eveready® battery." Also, by doing a little research, I realized that we had to do much more planning, scheduling, and compromising to keep our sex life afloat during the active parenting season of marriage.

Dave

---

treat each other. Ask yourself, "Is our home generally a fun, happy place to be?" If you answer yes, your marriage is helping to set a positive tone, and your children will be benefactors!

3. Your Marriage Helps Shape Relationships

Think about your own parents and what you observed as you were growing up. What did your parents model to you? Were they loving and affectionate with each other? Huggers normally come from families of huggers. Usually you will have picked up many ways of relating that were taught to you (either consciously or not) by your parents.

The upside to all this is that if you work to build a strong, loving marriage, your children will, by watching you, learn how to give and receive love, how to nurture, how to resolve conflict, how to communicate, and how to live. These behaviors will be as natural to them as breathing and will be the foundation for all their future relationships. What a legacy to give your children!

Changing Through Doing!

"The greatest help you gave us during your Marriage Alive seminar was raising our 'faith level.' You convinced us that we could take one little step to improve our love life. We did it, and that encouraged us to take another. Before long our attitude changed from one of despair to hope. Thanks!"

Seminar participant

CHANGING FOCUS

$\mathcal{G}$reat!" one parent lamented. "I see the need for time for myself, my marriage, and my children, but I don't know where to start to find balance or refocus. Our children and their urgent needs just seem to take over!"

"A starting place," we told him, "is to analyze your learning style and how you best initiate change."

People initiate change in different ways—but everyone can learn and change! Some initiate change by first changing their attitude; others begin through acquiring knowledge; others need to just do something! Let's look closer at each.

Attitude

Some people change by first changing their attitude. They need to say, "Starting now, my spouse will be first in my life! I choose to do all I can to develop a more creative love life." This then motivates them to action.

Knowledge

Some people initiate change by gaining knowledge. Perhaps by reading this book, you will be more motivated to make your love life a high priority. Maybe you have never thought about the fact that your spouse will still be around after the children grow up and leave home. With this new insight you are eager to make changes.

Four Steps for Prioritizing Your Marriage

1. Recommit yourself to your marriage and acknowledge that it is worth investing in and cherishing.
2. Each day be alert to little ways you can put your marriage at a higher priority.
3. Nurture your marriage by finding time alone together and by concentrating on improving your love life.
4. Relinquish any guilt feelings you may have about taking time away from your children. Remember that they will also benefit from your renewed marriage focus.

Let Your Marriage Be Center Page!

"Late nights with sick children leave me burned out to the point of exhaustion. I find myself exhausted emotionally, mentally, and physically. But I have a loving, sensitive husband who cares for me and helps out around the house and with the children. It's so important that burdens are shared equally so that one of us doesn't get crazy! My advice is: Your kids need to know that they are not the center of the marriage and that you have other priorities besides them. They need to see a healthy, loving relationship between their parents. Take advantage of baby-sitting—an exchange program, if necessary. When we can, we try to be romantic, spontaneous, creative, and we always carry a condom!"

Survey participant

Action

Some people initiate change through doing—by taking action. If this describes you, you can initiate change by taking a step of faith and planning that date or romantic getaway. Just acting and doing something will help you change your attitude.

However you function best—by changing your attitude, gaining knowledge, or taking action—start today to make your marriage and your love life a high priority.

NOW IT'S YOUR TIME TO CHANGE

*N*ow—not when the kids grow up—is a wonderful time to take another step toward intimacy, toward building a deeper, more meaningful relationship. Now is the time to be the best person you can be. Is there an attitude you need to change? A subject you need to research? An action you need to take?

What the Experts Say

Child development specialists generally agree that the ideal set-ting for the healthy development of a child is two loving par-ents, mutually fulfilled in their marriage, who can provide their children with warm, nonpossessive love. John Bradshaw, in his book *Bradshaw on: The Family,* proposed that families should be viewed as systems, the chief component of which is the mar-ital partnership. If that is functioning well, the children will have the opportunity to grow up as happy, healthy people. A child identifies positively with the parent of his or her own sex and learns by observation how to relate positively to the parent of the opposite sex.[5]

When we seek to grow, change, learn, and adapt to each other, our love life will get better and better. Listen to one mom's comments: "We have noticed as we have been mar-ried longer, trust each other more, and know each other bet-ter that sex has gotten better. My husband just commented a few weeks ago, 'Every time we have sex, I don't think it could possibly be better than the last time, and it amazes me that it is!' That is a wonderful benefit of persevering!"

Prioritizing your marriage and uniting with your mate will help you put everything in its proper place. It will help you put life's little conflicts and trials in perspective. Together you can make time for each other. You can make time for sex. You *can* have kids and a love life too!

Four

~

Building Blocks
for Great Sex

*Y*ou didn't tell me how the third baby complicates your life!" Abby complained. "Just getting through the day is a major feat. Forget marriage goals or in-depth conversations. And did I mention writing deadlines? Having my own home-based editorial business sounded so clever. What insanity to think I could balance life, love, and the pursuit of anything!"

"Sure, it's hard now," Claudia responded. "But you can't put your marriage on hold!"

Focused on our intense discussion, we hardly noticed as Abby's three-year-old daughter, Sophie, played at our feet, stacking blocks. Then, almost as an exclamation point, Sophie kicked the foundational blocks, and the wobbly structure crashed to the floor.

"That's exactly how I feel," Abby exclaimed. "Our family is like a pile of blocks stacked precariously on top of each other. One false move and everything will crash!"

Can you identify with Abby? Life is spinning out of control. Why is it so hard to balance being a partner and parent? Traditional families are difficult enough, but managing blended families and second and third marriages is even more complicated. There are more blocks to balance.

What are the building blocks for your marriage? For your love life? Since you've had kids, are your blocks a little wobbly? Perhaps it's time for a checkup—time to make sure the foundational blocks of your relationship are solidly in place. Reaffirming the foundational blocks of your marriage and family will strengthen your relationship and provide a solid base for building a creative love life. We've identified five blocks that are at the base of every relationship: communication, conflict resolution, encouragement, shared core beliefs, and commitment to growth.

1. COMMUNICATION—WE NEED TO TALK

The most fundamental block of any relationship is the ability to communicate with each other. It impacts every aspect of your life—especially sex. From our survey we affirmed that you can have good communication and a lousy sex life, but it's next to impossible to have lousy communication and a great sex life.

On the other hand, most of those who said they had good marital communication were more satisfied with their sexual relationship. They also found it easier to talk about their love life.

If you don't talk about your sexual relationship, you're missing out on a whole dimension of your love life. As one of

Talk to Me!

"To me sex is just one more thing to do—something else that somebody needs. Once I get into it, I'm okay. But this takes a lot of mental preparation. I'm always thinking of what I have to do when I'm done. It would help if my husband would spend time just talking to me at other times!"

Survey participant

our psychologist friends said, "If you don't talk, think, or read about sex, you'll soon forget about it!" So how can you begin to talk about your love life? We have three tips: listen for feelings, talk about sex, and develop a sex vocabulary.

Listen for Feelings

At no time is it as important to listen for feelings as when you talk about sex. "Honey, I've got a headache" can be packed with many different messages. It may mean, "I have a headache," or it could mean several other things, such as:

- "You ignored me this morning, so I'm going to ignore you now."
- "I just don't have the energy or interest in sex right now."
- "Why can't you start with romance? Then I might be more interested in sex."
- "I need some time alone to myself before I can focus on anyone else."

Understanding the hidden messages behind words is hard. (Of course, sometimes there are no hidden messages.) But as you listen for feelings, observe body language, including posture, gestures, glances, and countenance. Mixed in with nonverbal communication may be that "come hither" look that tells you, "I'm in the mood for love!" But that love potential may simply remain potential unless you take our next tip.

Talk About Sex

"My husband, Ralph, just doesn't understand what turns me on," Lucy confided to us in one of our Marriage Alive seminars. "He's too rough. It's like he goes for the kill without giving me time to get into lovemaking."

We asked her, "Do you talk about your lovemaking? Do you tell him how you would like him to approach you?"

"Oh no," Lucy replied. "We never talk about it. We just do it."

The "just doing it" was not satisfying for either Ralph or Lucy. They desperately needed to talk to each other. From our observations as we have worked with couples over the years, Lucy and Ralph are not unique. Why do people who can talk for hours about their children find sex an embarrassing, off-limits topic? Maybe they tried to talk about sex but ended up criticizing or blaming each other. Also, since some of a man's self-esteem is connected to his sexual performance, maybe he fears being told he is not meeting his wife's expectations. Or maybe they want to talk about sex but just don't have the vocabulary!

These obstacles can be overcome. Simple communication skills will help you talk openly and honestly about your sex life without blaming or attacking each other. We've learned it helps to start our sentences with "I" and let them reflect back on the speaker. Lucy could say, "Honey, I need you to touch me tenderly before I can respond sexually. Hugs, kisses, and even telling me throughout the day how much you love me help me open up and respond to you."

The message Ralph would receive would be

Tips for Talking

- Start sentences with "I."
- Avoid "you" statements and "why" questions.
- Avoid the words "never" and "always." Absolute statements will get you in trouble!
- Give five positive statements for each negative statement.
- Generously use the words "please" and "thank you."
- Develop your own secret love language.

Our "Love Bird" Chirpy

Early in our marriage, before we had children, we had a parakeet named Chirpy. One evening we were at our neighbors' house. It was getting late, and all day Dave and I had been sending each other love signals. We knew it was time to head home. To initiate our departure, Dave said, "We need to go home now. It's time to feed Chirpy." Our friends saw right through us and laughed us out the door. Afterward, from time to time we referred to making love as "feeding Chirpy." Years later we still talk about "feeding the birds": "Honey, don't you think it's time to feed the birds?" "What about meeting for lunch and feeding the birds?" It's our private vocabulary!

Claudia

quite different from "You're too rough and hurry too much," "You aren't trying to please me at all!" "Why can't you be more gentle?" Avoiding "you" statements and "why" questions will help keep conversations positive and productive.

Develop a Sex Vocabulary

While hugs and kisses are an important part of your love language, you also need words. Remember, your mate is not a mind reader! If you rely only on the nonverbal, you will misread each other. For us developing a sex vocabulary was like learning to speak a new language—only this time *we* determined the meaning of the words!

Why not create your own intimate vocabulary? If you feel uncomfortable saying "penis" or "vagina," come up with your own special names. Among some other intimate terms we've heard are these creative ones: One wife referred to her husband's private parts as "Big Jim and the twins;" a husband wrote that he enjoyed his wife's twin peaks.

Poetry and music add to our love vocabulary and help us talk about loving our spouse. You can develop your vocabulary by reading books together. One survey participant shared this tip: "My husband and I read together *Mars and Venus in the Bedroom* by John Gray. Everything in the book wasn't for us, but it had some wonderful insights, and we learned a lot about each other's physical and emotional needs. We'd read a chapter and then go to bed! By the way, this was all my husband's idea!" Reading books can help you develop a love vocabulary. For example, highlight a passage that expresses your feelings. Then in the margin write, "Yes! That's me" or "Ditto." Eventually, using someone else's words to communicate your needs will give you the confidence to form your own words.

King Solomon's Sex Dictionary

King Solomon understood the importance of having a love vocabulary. Thousands of years ago he coined this love language in Song of Songs.

- "Your eyes are doves" (1:15).
- "He browses among the lilies" (2:16).
- "Your lips are like a scarlet ribbon" (4:3).
- "Your two breasts are like two fawns, like twin fawns of a gazelle" (4:5).
- "Your lips drop sweetness as the honeycomb, my bride; milk and honey are under your tongue" (4:11).
- "You are a garden ... [and] a well of flowing water" (4:12, 15).
- "Let my lover come into his garden and taste its choice fruits" (4:16).
- "His body is like polished ivory decorated with sapphires" (5:14).
- "His mouth is sweetness itself" (5:16).

2. CONFLICT RESOLUTION—WE NEED
TO WORK IT OUT

One seminar participant asked us, "If we start talking about sex, what do we do when we disagree?"

"You keep talking," we told him.

We are both strong-willed and opinionated. At times we totally disagree with each other—even about our sex life! Sometimes we misunderstand each other and get angry. But we don't have to stay angry. Years ago marriage enrichment pioneers Drs. David and Vera Mace taught us how to make an anger contract. We try to put that contract into immediate effect when either of us becomes angry. Basically, we have agreed to tell each other whenever we *begin* to get angry. This helps us deal with the situation before it escalates into a heated argument. Another part of our contract is that we will not attack each other or defend ourselves, and we will ask for each other's help in dealing with our anger and whatever is causing the anger.

> **Our Anger Contract**
> 1. We agree to tell each other when we are getting angry.
> 2. We agree not to vent our anger at each other.
> 3. We will ask for each other's help in solving whatever is causing the anger.[1]
>
> Signed: _____
> Signed: _____

In our survey we observed that when couples had difficulty resolving conflict, sexual satisfaction was also low, and vice versa. But when couples were skilled at handling conflict, they tended to have a great sexual relationship. So making an anger contract can benefit your love life. It will help you short-circuit your anger so you can work things out.

A Word of Caution

Relationships are fluid, and most couples are still in the process of developing ways to cope with anger, problems, conflict, and so on. If you need more help in processing anger and learning conflict resolution skills, we recommend two great books that deal extensively with conflict and anger in marriage: *Love and Anger in Marriage* by Dr. David Mace and *Fighting for Your Marriage* by Drs. Howard Markman, Scott Stanley, and Susan Blumberg.[2]

Your love life, like your marriage relationship, is continually changing. It's going forward or backward. It's a journey, not a destination. You don't suddenly arrive and have a great marriage with a great sex life. And wherever you are, you can move forward. One survey participant wrote, "It's often hard to remember that today is not the last day on earth we have to get it right, so we often go to bed feeling like things will never improve. Nothing drives healthy sexual intimacy further away than feelings of inadequacy. That is why we have to keep reminding each other to let the law of love be uppermost and to forgive each other for our shortcomings. By God's grace, there is always tomorrow to begin anew, and if we don't allow failure to saturate our souls, we can keep growing and can find our lovemaking to be a source of great strength and bonding."

Wise advice! Forgiving and accepting each other paves the way for a closer, more intimate love life.

3. ENCOURAGEMENT—WE NEED TO BUILD EACH OTHER UP

*W*ait a minute," one wife interrupted. "What do you mean by encouragement? If I encouraged my husband, I'd never get out of bed! How do you encourage a mate who is always ready?"

Another wife spoke up. "I'm married to a man who taught the Energizer bunny everything he knows, but I think encouragement means telling him that he satisfies me—in bed and out of bed."

Encouragement has two aspects. First, as a foundation for your relationship, encouragement is establishing patterns of support and praise that affirm each other's identity and worth. Second, as a foundation for your love life, encouragement is initiating sexual intimacy.

Establishing Patterns of Support and Praise

Everyone needs to feel loved and valued. How are you doing at affirming your mate? Did you know that it takes five positive statements to offset one negative statement?[3]

Areas to Affirm

Make a list of different aspects of your mate's life that you can affirm. Then write a note to your spouse and leave it in an unexpected but sure-to-be-found place. Some areas where your spouse may appreciate encouragement include:

- profession or employment
- parenting skills
- physical fitness (weight loss or staying fit)
- staying intellectually rigorous
- maintaining social obligations
- managing finances
- staying attractive
- growing spiritually
- creativity
- humor and ability to laugh

Listen to yourself for twenty-four hours and see what your ratio is. Develop the habit of affirming your spouse.

We often take for granted little things that our spouses do that enhance our relationships and families. Remember that a word of affirmation can do wonders for self-esteem and contentment.

Initiating Sexual Intimacy

Along with being able to communicate your sexual needs to your spouse, you may need to encourage a spirit of adventure and willingness to participate in regular sex. One therapist told us that half of his clients complain that their mates bother them all the time to have sex, and the other half complain that their mates never bother them. He said, jokingly, if he could shuffle the couples, everyone would be happy.

Your sex drives and expectations may be different. If you want your spouse to try something different or do something more frequently, you will need to give gentle encouragement. And this type of encouragement is needed all day long—not just when you're being intimate. A smile, a kiss, that certain look across the room, a phone call, leaving an unexpected "I love you" note, can all further your intimacy goals.

When we were first married, we used to make greeting cards for each other. We'd also let each other know what recent sexual experiences we particularly enjoyed and what we were looking forward to. While you may be short on time, look for ways to express encouragement to your mate. You can get great deals on Valentine cards on February 15! Stock up and send or hide Valentine cards through the year. You can add your own intimate message.

Another great tip from a survey participant is to note what your mate does to encourage you, then wait two or three weeks and encourage your mate in the same way! We're convinced that spouses cannot give each other too much genuine encouragement. Encouragement is like marital vitamins and will add energy and joy to your love life.

4. SHARED CORE BELIEFS—WE NEED SPIRITUAL INTIMACY

The birth of your first baby can shake the foundational blocks of your life. Before becoming parents, we had never paid much attention to our spiritual lives or our core beliefs. Then a difficult birth coupled with a baby who didn't immediately breathe launched our spiritual search.

We needed more than just sexual intimacy. We needed a spiritual intimacy that would add depth to our relationship, help us hold on when the storms of life appeared, and give us a purpose for living that was greater than the two—now three—of us.

We began to realize that the values and morals we held—our belief system—not only held us together, they

Create Your Own Deck of Love

Both of you write out cards saying how you would like to be encouraged. For example, "I like it when you

- rub my back at night"
- offer to put the kids to bed or clean the kitchen"
- fix my favorite dessert"
- whisper in my ear that you love me"
- hold my hand"
- call me for no reason"

Keep your cards in an obvious, convenient place. Each of you choose one each day as a memory jogger.

also affected our sexual relationship. Dr. Paul Pearsall, author of *Super Marital Sex,* reports, "Belief systems are as important, perhaps more important, to sexuality as any other area of life. Developing a shared belief system is central to super marital sex. This is why marriage offers a unique opportunity for intimacy, for it provides the time and opportunity for spiritual growth through life changes."[4]

This should not surprise us. God is the one who created us as sexual beings. He is the originator of sex and created us with the capacity for great sexual pleasure. In fact, those couples whose marriages have a spiritual dimension may be the most fulfilled sexually. Sociologist Andrew Greeley surveyed married people and found that couples who frequently pray together are twice as likely as those who pray less often to describe their marriages as being highly romantic. They also report considerably higher sexual satisfaction and more sexual ecstasy!

Spiritual Intimacy Developers
- Pray together.
- Worship together.
- Serve others together.
- Willingly forgive each other.

In building our marriage and especially in building a creative love life, we realized the importance of developing our own way to stay close to each other. So as we developed spiritual intimacy with God, we began to pray together. Having spiritual intimacy helped us open up to each other and share our most private hopes and fears in all areas of our lives. Our faith directly influences our love life, giving it a spiritual dimension. Andrew Greeley says that the sexual union is actually part of the sacrament of marriage.[5] In our core belief system, sex is a sacred trust given for our mutual pleasure. It is part of the glue that holds us together.

What is the glue that holds you together? How do your core beliefs affect your love life?

5. COMMITMENT TO GROWTH—WE NEED TO NURTURE OUR LOVE

Along with effective communication, the ability to resolve conflict, daily encouragement, and a shared core belief system, having a commitment to a growing marriage relationship is vital. Just as it takes two to have children, it takes two to have a growing marriage. Unfortunately, too many people have interpreted the marriage vow "till death do us part" as "until I'm not happy anymore." Without a commitment to both permanence and growth, marriages can die. Those marrying today will face a 60-percent possibility of divorce or permanent separation.[6]

How would you rate your commitment to your marriage? In what ways would you like to see your marriage grow and improve?

Listen for His Feelings!

Men and women often communicate differently, and sometimes it's hard to really hear and understand each other's emotions. One of the hardest things to do when I'm listening to Dave is to not make assumptions about what he's thinking or feeling. My advice? Be observant, but don't read too much into your husband's nonverbal cues. Before any serious conversation, agree to take each other at face value. When you think your husband's nonverbal message may be contradicting his words, gently ask him, "Tell me again how you really feel about this." Then really listen! You may be amazed at what you hear.

Claudia

Talking to Her about Sex

If you were like the majority of adolescent boys, when you were between the ages of twelve and eighteen, you probably thought about sex all the time. You talked about sex with your friends and developed an interesting vocabulary to refer to certain body parts or sexual acts. Thankfully, you have toned it all down now as an adult, but you still probably are more easily able than your wife to talk about sex.

While you were getting in trouble for the crass note you passed in the hallway, your wife was likely talking to her friends about how dreamy it was to hold a boy's hand, how her heart leaped when he looked at her, and how excited she was to go to the prom and what she would wear. Of course, teenage girls talk about sex, but usually not with the same explicitness or frequency as teenage boys. So don't be put off by your wife's seeming reluctance to tell you what pleases her or to ask for a specific sexual favor. Be patient with her and ask her direct questions to help her relate her preferences. Eventually you'll be using the same language.

Dave

Begin by affirming your commitment to having a growing love life and to working to maintain it through the parenting years. Obviously, at times we sacrificed for the critical needs of our children. But at other times we put their needs on hold and took care of our marriage. Over the years we were determined to get through the rough spots, to somehow work out a solution for our different sex drives, to continue to make time for loving each other, and to arrive at the empty nest with our love life intact. Because we didn't give up during the hectic parenting years, we are finding that this is the best stage of life yet! But even in the empty nest we have to guard and invest in our love life.

Investing in your love life is hard work, as one survey participant affirmed: "We've been married for eleven years, and most of that time my husband has worked evenings and nights. One way we've stayed connected is each year I buy a small bound notebook and leave him a note before I go to bed. Sometimes I let him know how my day went, a cute thing one of our three boys said or did, bits of information like, 'wake me up to snuggle.'

"I have one rule: I don't tell him about an unresolved issue or something that would cause him to worry or get upset—those things are kept for open discussion. I always say, 'I love you.' Over the years he has let me know how much he appreciates the notes—especially when I may forget to leave one. It is something small that I have come to enjoy that builds our relationship. It's also a journalizing of our years together—a model perhaps for our sons to follow."

~

*O*nce your marital building blocks are in place, the next step is to talk about your expectations for your love life. We'll look at that step in the next chapter.

Five

~

Expectations—
His and Hers

*O*ur friends Jenny and David are avid readers, so when the latest historical novel hits their favorite bookstore, they are there to pick up their copy. But being the frugal-minded couple that they are, Jenny and David usually share a copy instead of buying two books. This really shouldn't be a problem for them, since they keep such different hours. Jenny likes to read before her bedtime—9:00 P.M.—while David usually has two or three more hours to go before he ends his evening. Their problem isn't *sharing* the book; it's *talking* about it the next day. You see, they don't read at the same pace. So when Jenny comments on some aspect of the thickening plot, David cries out, "Don't tell me about that; I'm not there yet!"

Crafting a love life is much like sharing a novel; for it to be mutually enjoyable, you have to work at the same pace—read off the same page. Rare is the couple, however, who want the same things in a love life, the same types of pleasure in the same quantities. More typical is two people with very different likes and expectations trying their best to sort out a satisfying middle ground, and then complicating the process by becoming parents.

During a seminar session on having a creative love life, one mom asked, "Romance must be for people without kids. How can anyone have an exciting sex life after children come along?"

"I know what you mean," another participant added. "You have to factor in lack of time, energy, privacy, and then on those rare occasions when I do feel amorous, my husband is not interested, or there's a child asleep in our bed!"

"Just because you have children," we told the group, "doesn't mean you can't have romance or be a creative lover, but you will have to work harder at it. You also have to talk through your expectations. You need to get on the same page."

"But what if your page is blank?" asked another seminar participant.

As the group laughed, we responded, "You have to start somewhere! Actually, it's not a bad idea to start with a blank page. Erase your unrealistic expectations and start fresh!"

IN SICKNESS AND IN HEALTH

*H*aving kids and a love life too takes extra effort. When things don't work out as planned, you have to persevere. For example, to celebrate our twentieth anniversary, Dave planned a romantic getaway. He reserved the honeymoon suite—complete with a heart-shaped spa and a dozen red roses.

There we were, standing on the threshold of one of the most romantic anniversary settings. But it wasn't to be. "It's just not fair!" Claudia said, fighting back tears. "Everything is so perfect—why did this happen to us?"

Dave responded, "I know. It's a real bummer! Certainly not what I planned, but we'll have other times in the future."

Claudia, feeling little comfort, grabbed the roses. Taking one last glance at the untouched room just waiting for us to enjoy it, we closed the door, got in our car, and started the drive home to Knoxville and our youngest son, who was sick with the flu. Missed expectations. Hope deferred until who knows when! Real life at the Arps'.

Later that evening we spent a quiet anniversary with Jonathan. "Remember the words in our wedding liturgy, 'in sickness and in health'?" Dave asked. "Well, it should include 'and when your kids have the flu, too.'"

We don't know about your kids, but ours seemed to have a radar that signaled, "Mom and Dad have plans—it's time to get sick, fall off a jungle gym, or run into a barbed-wire fence while playing soccer!" If you have kids, count on interruptions!

At other times our own sicknesses have ruined great romantic plans, like the time we finally got away to the House on the Metolious, one of our favorite romantic spots, located in the mountains near Sisters, Oregon. This time it wasn't so romantic. Dave had bronchitis and couldn't lie down without having a coughing attack. He ended up sleeping on the couch.

And what about the everyday things that wipe out the best laid plans? The baby wakes up after sleeping only fifteen minutes, or your daughter gets chicken pox and has to be picked up at school the morning you both planned to stay home for a couple of hours, or your mate falls asleep in the recliner while reading the paper the night you had a romantic evening planned. Many times circumstances beyond our control create havoc with our expectations. Sometimes it's not that we're not on the same page—we aren't even reading the same book!

BUT I THOUGHT …

Without a doubt, the most frustrating situations have been when we misread each other's expectations. This usually happens when we don't talk about them. We must confess this still happens to us—even as we write this chapter.

We often combine writing with our travels, and we look for blocks of time in isolated settings. We love to get away from the phone, fax, and people. As we write this chapter, we are in the Black Forest of southern Germany. We are so far from civilization that it took us a week to find a place to send and receive e-mail!

Writing a book about "no time or energy for sex" when we have all the time and energy in the world can be very pleasant. We've done our share of research. However, we still misread each other's expectations.

A couple of days ago we were getting ready to go for a walk. Claudia noticed that Dave had not shaved. Rather than speak up, Claudia thought, "He thinks I'm not interested in sex today, so he doesn't care how he looks!"

Dave, with hidden amorous feelings, thought, "We'll just get hot and sweaty on our walk. I'll get cleaned up and shave afterward. Maybe we'll shower together."

Claudia thought, "I wish he would shave. It's been fun to stop along the way as we walk, and kiss like we did years ago when we were dating and hiked in the Smoky Mountains. Guess he doesn't care!"

Dave silently wondered, "What's bugging Claudia? She must not be interested in sex today!"

Finally we realized something was going on. We were on different pages. When we told each other what we assumed, we realized we were both wrong. We never outgrow our need to identify and understand each other's expectations!

IDENTIFYING EXPECTATIONS

*T*o craft a fulfilling love life, you need to identify your expectations. Basically, you must know two things:

what you want out of a love life and what ṭ
wants out of a love life.

Not that easy, is it? We carry so much ba
that sorting out what is truly important to us in a love ....
a confusing process. Perhaps you have a media-created image
of what your love life should be like. Movies, soap operas,
magazine articles, and sensual commercials are deadly when
it comes to portraying unrealistic images of a satisfying love
life. Or maybe you grew up with such a stigma concerning
sex before marriage that you are having a tough time believ-
ing that sex and pleasure are appropriate after marriage.

You must understand your own needs and desires and
express them in order to give your partner the opportunity
to meet them. To expect your partner to read your mind is
unfair. Plus, when your partner does not meet your unspo-
ken needs, you may feel unfulfilled and rejected, and you
may let your emotions affect other areas of the marriage
relationship. If, however, you take the time to sort out your
needs and desires and then use the communication tools we
have previously discussed to talk about them, a truly wonderful and fulfilling sex life can unfold.

Talking about your sexual expectations is one of the
most intimate times you will ever share with your spouse
and should be initiated in an atmosphere of trust, unconditional love, and acceptance. We realize there will be differences in your desires and in how adventurous you are. One
caution: if one partner is having difficulty expressing his or
her expectations, be patient, gentle, and accepting.

We have three tips to help you begin to talk about your
expectations: (1) be verbal, (2) be specific, (3) be realistic.

1. Be Verbal

One of the greatest things you can do for your love life is
to talk about your expectations. You may want to talk first

Talking It Over

To help you talk about your expectations, complete the following sentences. Then share your answers with each other.

• When I think of intimacy and closeness I _____

_____

• My idea of romance is _____

_____

• I feel the most sexual fulfillment when you _____

_____

• I know our sexual desires correspond when we _____

_____

about the best aspects of your love life and then the major obstacles you need to overcome. Talking about your expectations will help you understand each other and get on the same page. Don't be surprised if your expectations are different. Really, you should probably be surprised if they are the same. Talking about your expectations can be a great starting point for better understanding each other's needs and desires.

2. Be Specific

When identifying what you want out of your relationship, be specific. Discuss the following questions.

• How often would you like to have intercourse?
• How much hugging and cuddling do you need before intercourse? (Put it in minutes if necessary.)
• Do you need romance to set the mood?
• What are the fantasies you have been hoping to fulfill with me?

This exercise may sound a little individualistic and crass, but it is necessary. You are working toward the goal of a mutually fulfilling love life, which means you must know what will fulfill you and what will fulfill your spouse.

Of course, being realistic about your needs and expectations means that you may have to save some items for special getaways and that you may have to prioritize your wishes. Now it's time to pull out your calendar and sched-

> **Here's What I Would Like!**
>
> Both of you make a list of your desires and expectations. Then categorize the items on each other's lists, using the number system below.
>
> 1. No way, never.
> 2. You might be able to talk me into it.
> 3. I'll bargain with you on that one.
> 4. Sure, that's easy.
> 5. It would be my pleasure!

ule a month's worth of mutually agreed-upon pleasuring. (Important: use codes if your kids—or worse yet, your parents—might see the calendar!)

If scheduling sex seems unrealistic or forced, or if you aren't sure you'll have any energy for all this, don't despair. We'll be talking about these issues in later chapters. You can always finish this exercise later. But we still want you to discuss your expectations and desires, because it will give you an incentive to fit sex and romance into your life.

3. Be Realistic

Each season of marriage offers challenges and opportunities for growth, and in each season you will need to reexamine your expectations. What is realistic in one season may be totally unrealistic at another time. Here is how we see those seasons as we look back over our thirty-five years of marriage.

Early Marriage Years: Discovering How to Love Each Other

We were married for four years before our first son was born. Balancing college and work wasn't easy, but we found time for loving each other, for discovering our individual sexual likes and dislikes. We found that the more we talked about our expectations, the less inhibited we were. We read books, we experimented, and we discovered what worked for us.

Pleasure Calendar

Plan a month's worth of pleasure together. Note the days you have set aside for loving and include the specific types of pleasure you would like to try. Do your best to stick to your schedule, and plan in advance for any baby-sitting you'll need.

What was early marriage like for you? Maybe you're still there! Talking about the expectations and experiences you had when you were first married will help you get on the same page now. What in your early love life did you enjoy that you no longer do? Having the same level of spontaneity as you did before you had children is not realistic, but perhaps in your times of "planned pleasure" you could include some things you did before the children were born.

Baby and Toddler Years: Helping Our Love Life Survive

Realistic sexual expectations at this stage of family life may simply be maintenance and survival! We've already discussed how that first baby complicates your love life. And before you know what's happened, everything else seems to come first—the baby, your career advancement, your friends, your social life. Sex can become an obligation or something you just don't think about. It is vital that you talk about your expectations and devise a workable plan—even if you are totally exhausted!

Our expectations were different—even in the way we handled exhaustion! When Claudia was exhausted, she was totally exhausted. No life in that woman until her battery was recharged with sleep and rest. Dave could be as exhausted as Claudia, but he had a spare "Eveready battery." Gender differences seem to be most pronounced during this stage of family life. Mothers (like Claudia) especially run low on energy.

However tired you are, don't give up on your love life, but do be flexible and responsive. Do talk about your expectations and be realistic. This is a great time to make a list of ways to romance your mate in ten minutes or less. Realize that some things will work and other things won't.

Middle Parenting Years: Renewing Expectations for Our Love Life

When all the children went to school at the same time, it was a great day for us! We looked forward to having relief

---

Hormones Affect Love Life

The hormonal changes a woman goes through during pregnancy, nursing, and even your monthly cycle can greatly alter your desire for sex. And although it may seem obvious to you that sex is out of the question on any given night (due to fatigue or other factors), don't assume that your spouse is picking up your signals. Communicate to your spouse that your lack of interest in sex is based more on physiological issues than on a lack of desire or love for him. Share with him chapters in your parenting books that talk about the changes in sexual desire during these times and how there is hope for resuming normal relations when your hormones level out again.

---

from twenty-four-hour parenting, and we anticipated more flexibility in our schedule and more opportunities to revitalize our love life, which was stuck in a survival mode.

Change isn't easy. Transition times can be risky. Initially we had differing expectations and differing ideas about how to reinvent our love life. For instance, our body clocks are different. But as we experimented, we discovered lovemaking was not just reserved for nighttime. With some creative scheduling, we managed to carve out time each week to meet at home without the kids around. It was a sex-life saver for us, and we often recommend daytime sex to parents in our seminars.

"I just couldn't have sex during the day," a seminar participant told Claudia during a break. "It just wouldn't seem right."

"Why not?" Claudia asked.

"Well, I'm not sure I could gear down in the middle of the day. I always have my list of twenty things that need to be done, and I just don't think I could get in the mood."

In Ten Minutes or Less You Can ...

- leave romantic messages on your partner's answering machine
- place a flower or love note under his or her windshield wiper
- pick up your mate's favorite candy bar when you're grocery shopping
- send a card thanking your spouse for being your lover, friend, soul mate
- give your partner a foot massage
- put a note on the TV saying, "Forget the television. You've already turned me on!"
- have a "quickie"

Hotel Getaway

"We came up with a creative idea that works great for our family. Each month we plan a getaway at a local hotel. Since we come each month, they willingly give us a 9:00 A.M. check-in time. So we spend the day as a family and splash in the swimming pool and use their weight room. Sometimes we watch a movie. Our kids love it and leave happily when the sitter picks them up late in the afternoon. Then we have the rest of the evening and the next morning without the kids. It's something we look forward to each month!"

Survey participant

Reality check: our kids would have probably left complaining—but they would have left!

Dave and Claudia

"I remember feeling the same way," Claudia told her. "But my list always waited for me. If I just took the first step, it was amazing how my attitude could change. Those daytime rendezvous became important to both of us. At least give it a try!"

Her husband agreed! As they talked about their expectations, they designed their own game plan. You can, too. Your schedules might not be as flexible as ours, but with flextime and personal days, perhaps you can leave a few hours late for work or take a long lunch! As you talk about your expectations, you'll discover realistic, creative ways to find time together.

During this season of life it is realistic to leave your children overnight. Finding friends willing to take your children for an evening in return for the same favor is easier now that the children are older. (Also, you can take advantage of school trips and activities.) How often would you like to get away? For how long? Twenty-four hours? A full weekend?

A week? Talk, brainstorm, compromise. Agree on what is realistic for you.

Adolescent Parenting Years: Holding On to Expectations for Our Love Life

Stress reappeared at the Arps' in the adolescent years! Talk about misunderstood expectations—and they weren't all concerning our love life. In a marriage there are few times more stressful than when you have teenagers in the house. First of all, they seem to stay up later than you do, leaving you little privacy. Second, someone is always having a crisis. It's easy to get so overwhelmed with their problems that you ignore your own.

> **Motto for the Adolescent Years**
>
> "When the kids are away, the parents will play!"

For us it was critical during these years to talk about our wants, desires, and expectations. To hang on to our love life, we simply had to focus and not let our teenagers zap all our emotional energy. We claimed Saturday mornings as "our time." Because our teenagers happily slept until noon, we found some privacy. So during this time talking about adolescent issues was forbidden.

Also, we looked for opportunities to get away overnight—like when everyone was off on a school trip. And we maximized the times when everyone was out of the house at football games or other sports or school activities. Fortunately, we knew "this too would pass." And our kids did finally grow up and leave home!

Your kids will also grow up. So our advice is to hang on, keep talking about your expectations, and plan as many getaways during this time as you can. Don't let your concern about your teenagers' sexuality affect yours. We have often

How to Increase Her Confidence

Letting your wife know how attractive and cherished she is to you is especially important as your children grow up and as the two of you age. The time when children start leaving the nest can be difficult for couples. Many relationships end. Don't let the seed of insecurity enter your wife's mind. Continually reassure her of your love and desire for her. Affirm your commitment to her, and you will increase her confidence and her desire for loving you in return.

Dave

---

observed a subtle change in friends when their kids reach the teenage years. They become more serious and joke less with us. Whatever you do, keep your sense of humor. This too shall pass!

The Empty Nest: Reviving Our Love Life

If you hang in there through the active parenting years, you can reap the benefits in the empty nest! Unfortunately, too often by the time couples get to this marriage milestone, they have no real love life. In the hilarious movie *Father of the Bride II*, the Barnes's pregnant daughter and son-in-law were appalled that the Barneses were also having a baby, which meant they still had sex!

Again, the key to a great sex life is being on the same page with your expectations. Talk, explore, and get ready for fun. The whole house will be yours again! You will have privacy. You should be more comfortable and enjoy each other more than ever. But still you must make sex a priority, or other things will walk right into your lives and crowd it out.

One day your children will grow up. If you keep talking about your expectations and keep seeking to meet each other's needs, if you are realistic in what you want in each

Find a Marriage Mentor

The first years of marriage bring many adjustments. Years ago when marriages were arranged by parents, the culture provided time for the new husband and wife to adjust to each other. In biblical times that period lasted for a year. Part of the culture was that when a man took a new wife, he was deferred from military duty and was not charged with any business for one full year!

Not so today. Little help is given to newlyweds. Some young couples have never really seen an enriched marriage. Many come from broken homes or from homes in which romantic love died long ago. Everyone needs models and mentors. Do you have an older couple with whom you can talk with who have an enriched marriage and love life? If not, find a couple who can be your mentor. Consider family, friends, and coworkers. Maybe you can become a mentor for a younger couple.

season of family life, you can be lifelong lovers—you can have a creative, enjoyable, functioning love life! In the next chapter we will give you a menu so you can talk about your sexual desires. You can get on the same page—and it can be a great love story!

Six

Love à la Carte

"Sex isn't as important as bread and water," one husband in our survey commented, "but it's right up near the top of the list!" Others used "food hunger" word pictures when referring to sex. Over and over we read, "Our sexual appetites are different!"

Whatever your sexual appetite, talking about sex and intimacy can be awkward. Women may have difficulty talking about sex, while men may struggle when talking about intimacy. A healthy love diet contains both.

At different stages of a marriage, your appetite may change, but keep talking. Long, relaxing gourmet sex may be a rare treat in the early parenting years. But even during those hectic years you need a balanced diet. Fast food has its place, but if that's all there is, your diet may lack important marital vitamins. To achieve a balanced love diet, talk about your likes and dislikes. We designed a menu—love à la carte—to help you do just that.

As you look through our menu, think about what sounds appetizing to you. What would your partner enjoy? Choose your own menu and be willing to talk about it.

Remember, if you want to have a satisfying and nutritious diet, compromise is important. Also remember that an à la carte menu is just that. Pick and choose selections that sound appetizing to both. If something sounds too kinky, please skip it! We are quite traditional, and while our love life is alive and well, some of the suggestions we read in books cause us to look at each other and say, "No way! Don't even think about it!"

Identifying and communicating your expectations is essential to a healthy love life. Our love à la carte menu will help you voice expectations and select a healthy diet of intimacy and sex.

We have divided our menu into appetizers, snacks and fast foods, main courses, and desserts.

APPETIZERS

Appetizers create interest, increase appetite, and precede a main course. They should

- be light
- be easy to prepare
- please the taste buds
- whet your appetite for the main course

An appetizer is a come-on, an invitation. We still remember sitting at Kelly's restaurant just south of Myrtle Beach, South Carolina. We had pulled the ultimate coup and slipped away from our three sons for a getaway. Our appetizer started with our feet under the table and that certain look. We held hands, while our feet had their own agenda. In the parking lot we kissed before heading back to our condo. Our drive back had its intimate moments, which we won't describe. When we got to our condo, we sat in our car and continued to kiss and cuddle. One thing led to another. We remember that evening for its great sex, but the great sex was preceded by great appetizers!

At home with the kids, an appetizer might be a phone call to say, "I love you," "I'm thinking about you"; a love note in a briefcase; one long-stemmed red rose; a gift of your favorite perfume or aftershave; or sitting on the couch, talking and listening to your favorite music after the kids are in bed.

> **Appetizers**
> - A back rub
> - A shower for two in a candlelit bathroom
> - A playful hug, embrace, or caress
> - A romantic movie shared together
> - A handwritten love note

Appetizers don't always immediately lead to the main course. They can actually function as an appetite depressant. They can make the main course much more enjoyable by tempering sexual cravings for the hungry partner and increasing desire for the one who isn't so hungry!

"But does an appetizer on your menu always include sexual intercourse?" one seminar participant asked.

"Usually not," we said, and we saw relief spread across her face. "Basically, an appetizer is anything that increases your desire and pleasure." Think about those things your spouse does that create interest and sexual tension.

What about hugs and kisses? For us they are great appetizers. Dr. Clifford and Joyce Penner agree. In their fun book *52 Ways to Have Fun, Fantastic Sex*, they write, "Kissing is an indicator of the quality of a sexual relationship. When kissing is passionate, warm, and deep, and when it's an ongoing part of a couple's relationship, they likely have a satisfying sexual relationship."[1] Sex can become so goal oriented that long, passionate kisses disappear and with them, some of the pleasure and intimacy a couple has known. So keep kissing!

SNACKS AND FAST FOODS

Snacks and fast foods alleviate hunger for a brief period of time. They are a quick treat, a mini-meal. Snacks and fast foods should

- be easy to prepare
- not totally appease the appetite or be the total diet
- taste good

Snacks are similar to appetizers but more often actually include the act of making love. In the parenting years, it's easy to get stuck on fast-food sex.

In their early years men have a quicker response time than women, and they tend to have more sexual tension to

The Best "Getting in the Mood" Tips from Parents

- "Flirt with each other—even when there isn't time for sex, make sure your mate knows you want to. If you communicate your desire, it keeps the passion fires smoldering."
- "It is possible to keep up a nice amount of tension, using paralanguage and little whispers, which help to keep the mood going until we are free to do something about it. This is a good way to prepare mind and body and also helps push out unwanted emotions that may try to intrude in the interim."
- "Spend time talking about the day, and if possible pray together."
- "Take a short walk together and hold hands."
- "Relax with a cup of tea. Turn off the TV."
- "Let your mate know that you want to spend time alone with him or her, that he or she is the center of the universe for you at this moment."

Why not have an appetizer date and talk about what is appetizing to you? You could make your own list.

release. Men compartmentalize sex; women don't. It takes women much longer to gear up for sex and to get into the mood. Remember, women need love and intimacy to give sex. Men need sex to give love and intimacy. When your needs are different, consider accommodating each other with a snack.

> **Snacks and Fast Foods à la Love**
>
> • A quickie
> • Ten minutes of non-demand touching
> • Only pleasuring one partner
> • A midnight or early-morning surprise
> • Old-fashioned petting (if you don't know what that is, ask your mother)

One snack we simply call the "quickie." It's when she says, "Honey, I'm just not up to a main course tonight, but what about a quickie?" It may be a time when one spouse is just too exhausted or has no huge appetite for sex. At times like these giving a gift of love and willingly meeting the needs of the other spouse with attentiveness and affection is a snack that can build intimacy and closeness in a marriage.

Giving quickies from time to time helps stomp out "faking it." Pretending to respond when you aren't responding is detrimental to your relationship. It is deceptive and destroys intimacy.

Snacks may be more important for one spouse than for the other. Dave remembers one weekend getaway when our children were really small and his sexual appetite was really big. "On Friday night when we got to the mountain cabin, we were both tired. Claudia, being a morning person, was more tired than I was, but she gladly agreed to a quickie. This relieved my sexual tension so that for the rest of the weekend I could concentrate on pleasing her, and together we crafted a weekend menu that was satisfying and pleasing for both of us."

Other fast-food times may be quick sex in the morning before the kids wake up, or a quick romp in the laundry room as you are folding clothes! One wife said it was great fun to make love on top of the vibrating washer and dryer. (Don't think that would work for us, but whatever invigorates your love life is what you need to try.) In one Marriage Alive seminar we suggested making love in different places in the home when the kids weren't around. One of the participants suggested the dining-room table. Later one of the couples in that seminar tried it, and their table broke! Their escapade gives new meaning to the term "safe sex."

MAIN COURSES

Main courses satisfy hunger, give energy and strength, and provide nutrients and vitamins needed for health and growth. Main courses should

- be well-balanced
- not be consumed too quickly
- have variety
- be appetizing to both
- satisfy deep hunger

Main courses take time and usually require planning. Remember, at this stage of life planning for sex and intimacy is what it's all about! Bob and Rosemary Barnes, in their book *Great Sexpectations,* write, "Lovemaking needs to be prepared for like a special event."[2] They encourage couples to set aside time in which each partner focuses on the other and on the other's dreams.

While every time you make love will not and cannot be a main course, for a healthy love diet you need planned times. An excellent way to plan a main course is to schedule an appointment. One survey participant agreed: "We usually have to make an appointment. When you can't have the privacy you want when you want it, make an appointment and be prepared to stick to it unless physical illness precludes intimacy."

When planning main courses, avoid ruts. Even your favorite entrée becomes taste-

> **Main Courses à la Love**
> - An evening of uninterrupted loving (send the kids to grandma's)
> - An afternoon at a hotel
> - A long lunch
> - A twenty-four-hour getaway

less if that's all you ever eat, so as one survey participant said, "Don't get stuck in a rut. Any time of day or night needs to remain an option. Get away alone for a night or two frequently."

Scheduling Sex

To add main courses to your already busy life, go on and make that love calendar. As you work around the distractions of meetings, athletic events, and social commitments, don't forget the one that comes monthly! One mom wrote, "When we plan for special times, I take into consideration that my level of sexual interest varies quite a bit according to my monthly cycle. We don't plan special 'events' or getaways for my low times."

Write on your calendar when you will have sex. As another wife put it, "It's difficult to find time, but planning helps. Setting a date makes it possible. It gives you time to plan and gives you something to look forward to." This will also encourage you to find sitters, make reservations, and designate funds for those main events. (In chapter 10 we will discuss in more detail how to schedule time for intimacy.) Why not make a list of main courses that sound appetizing to both of you?

Another wrote, "Nighttime isn't the only time, and your bedroom isn't the only appropriate place, for lovemaking. Using good judgment, discretion, and imagination can lead to a lot of fun. Go to a motel one night or go camping. Parents need time out, too."

DESSERTS

Desserts complete a wonderful meal, satisfy a sweet tooth, and bring little pleasures. Desserts should

- be special
- complement the main course
- not always be necessary

After a main course, desserts give love and intimacy that is so important—especially to the woman. (It's also important to the man, but he may not realize it.) Also, from time to time desserts are simply desserts and may not include the act of sex but definitely sweeten the relationship. What kinds of desserts do you like? They can be light or rich or even gourmet.

Desserts
- Verbally expressing affection
- Ten minutes of afterplay
- Two cups of tea and love talk
- Snuggling and holding each other before going to sleep
- Lying on a blanket and gazing at the stars

SETTING THE TABLE

Years ago Claudia made a great discovery. Even when we were eating leftovers, if she set an attractive table, the meal tasted better. Candlelight can even make peanut butter and jelly sandwiches taste good! This principle also works in our love life. For instance, when we lived in Europe, most places were underheated in the winter, so we traveled with our little red electric space heater. We can't tell you the difference that made in our love life!

What will set a lovely atmosphere for you and your spouse? Just remember, whatever menu you plan, how you serve it can add to the pleasure.

PLAN YOUR OWN MENU

Equipped with a few good ideas, your own imagination, and your own needs and desires, you should now be able to create a mutually satisfying trial menu. As we suggested in this chapter, plot out a month's worth of pleasuring and go to it. Afterward note what items you both enjoyed and what items you'd rather send back to the kitchen. And remember that your tastes will change from time to time. Just keep talking to each other and the rest will follow.

> **Set the Table for Love**
> - Candlelight
> - Romantic music
> - Perfume
> - Incense
> - Flowers
> - Silk pajamas and silk sheets
> - Your own portable electric heater!

King Solomon, the wise lover, understood the value of a smorgasbord of love. He is the one who penned, "He has brought me to his banquet hall, and his banner over me is love."[3] Now that you've planned your banquet of love, how do you find the time to carry out your plans? We'll show you in the next chapter.

Seven

~

No Time for Sex

My husband is in graduate school, both of us work full-time, and now we're parents—setting aside time to be together is difficult. We have a two-and-a-half-year-old. I'm away from home eleven hours a day, so when I get home, I feel the need to spend time with our son. After feeding and bathing him, I'm exhausted. I can't enjoy time with my husband, knowing I'm taking time away from my son, so the time I spend with my husband is usually after our son is in bed, which is late. It's hard on our sex life."

~

We consider ourselves pretty lucky. My wife has taken a break from her career to stay home with our kids during their preschool years. But we still never seem to have any time together. I have a pretty demanding career, and we thought she would be able to manage the household responsibilities, finances, church and social obligations, while still giving our kids the time they need. Boy, were we wrong. After my thirteen-hour days I can barely see straight, let alone help out at the house. And after spending the day with our four- and two-year-old kids with no breaks, my wife is physically and emotionally exhausted. We usually just pop on the TV and fall asleep on the sofa. So much for working on our love life."

～

*P*retty typical of most couples with young children, these survey respondents give voice to the most common complaint we hear about lacking a love life: "We just don't have any time!"

Even though life today is more hectic than it was when we had toddlers, we can remember the difficulties of balancing responsibilities, overcoming time constraints, and battling fatigue. We have already related some of the adjustments we made after our first child was born. The second child put even more pressure on our love life. We were living in Atlanta, Georgia, and were nearer to family but too far away to get help with baby-sitting. Dave worked for a computer company and traveled much of the time. When he came home, he was eager to get together. Claudia was exhausted and wanted help with our two boys, time out of the house, and, most of all, conversation!

While we loved each other and were committed to each other, our needs and desires were not the same. Dave wanted physical intimacy. Claudia wanted emotional intimacy. It wasn't an issue of finding ten minutes here and there for sex. What we needed was to find time for our total relationship. We had to talk about our expectations and how to use the little time we had. Claudia had to give a bit, and Dave had to be a little more realistic at that stage of parenting. Number-three son just added to our time deficiency.

Whatever stage of life you're in, finding time for building a creative love life will always be an issue. We all have to deal with the sex zapper that some call the "hurry sickness"—just too much to do and too little time to do it. All parents are susceptible. But let us give you this warning: Don't get so busy that you neglect your sex life. Once the system is shut down, it's hard to restart a love life, and in the future it could be more important to you than it is now. From our research (and personal experience) we discovered that the sexual relationship actually can be more satisfying in your forties than it was in your twenties. According to a 1994 University of Chicago study, women in their twenties are least likely to achieve orgasm during intercourse. Women in their early forties are most likely! One reason for this is that a man's response time slows down as he ages, while a woman's response time speeds up.[1]

HOW MUCH TIME DO YOU NEED?

*H*ow much time do you need for a love life? Remember, you need time not only for making love but also for building intimacy. So our answer is, you need as much time as you can make—not find! Finding time is circumstantial; making time is intentional. Let us give you some practical suggestions to help you capture time for you and your spouse.

Steps for Making Time for Sex

We've identified five steps for making time for sex: (1) make a commitment, (2) analyze your current time constraints, (3) set apart time for your marriage, (4) use your time twice, and (5) guard your time.

1. Make a Commitment

"Time for sex" has more to do with your attitude than your circumstance. We make time for those things that are the most important to us. To see what your priorities are, look at what you do with your discretionary time and money. How long has it been since you hired a baby-sitter just so you could have uninterrupted time together? Make a commitment to make time for sex.

2. Analyze Your Current Time Constraints

Keep a record for one week. How much time do you spend at different activities? How much time is nondiscretionary? For instance, the hours you work are probably not very flexible. Next list those things that must be done but the time frame for doing them is more flexible—household responsibilities, children's activities, meal preparation, and so on. Now think about the discretionary things you do. How much time do you spend each week watching television and videos, reading the paper, golfing, playing tennis or racquetball, or surfing the Internet? How much time do you spend with family and friends?

Now let us meddle. How much time do you spend each week with your mate? Thinking about your mate? Making love? How often do you have dates? How much time do you spend talking with your spouse?

Can you identify "time zappers"? What about television and videos? If you don't believe they are time zappers, just go into a video store on Friday afternoons and observe families who are walking out loaded down with videos. Paul Pearsall addresses this problem in *Super Marital Sex:* "TV addiction is one of the most detrimental influences on American marriages. It is a shared addiction, which is the worst type, because it sometimes covertly robs the relationship of available time for intimacy, while both partners take unknowing part in the theft."[2]

Analyze the data you have collected; you will probably see blocks of time you can claim for your love life! Now invest them!

3. Set Apart Time for Your Marriage

Set apart specific times dedicated to your spouse. They may be short or long.

- *Five-second hugs and kisses.* Each time you leave and come home, claim five seconds to hug and kiss. Never mind if you are running late. Five more seconds will not matter as much as your love life does!
- *Ten minutes to share.* David and Vera Mace taught us to have a ten-minute sharing time each day, when we don't try to have sex or solve problems but just touch emotionally. This has been invaluable, and we strongly recommend it to you!
- *Weekly date nights.* A regular date night will add immensely to your love life. This standing date is not necessarily for sex. And you don't even have to go out. Just carve out some time when you can otherwise occupy your children and have private time as a couple. (For dating suggestions see our books *10 Great Dates to Revitalize Your Marriage* [Zondervan, 1997] and *52 Dates for You and Your Mate* [Nelson, 1993].)

> **Two Love Rendezvous**
>
> - Meet at a restaurant. Go in separate cars. Pretend you haven't seen each other for several weeks.
> - For intrigue, invite your mate to meet you at a hotel. Give him or her the room number and time to arrive. Use your imagination for how you want to surprise your honey!

- *Twenty-four-hour getaways.* Regular getaways during the parenting years helped to keep our love life energized. During those brief rendezvous we were able to enjoy the spontaneity that just didn't happen at home with three boys underfoot! We realize this is an extremely difficult thing to pull off with young children, but make it a goal to get away together at least three times a year. (In chapter 12 we will give tips for pulling off getaways.)

- *Candlelit dinners for two.* Twice a month put the kids to bed early and have a romantic dinner at home.

4. Use Your Time Twice

Think of ways you can incorporate loving into your daily routine.

- Start a ritual of always making up the bed together each morning and sharing loving thoughts to carry each other through the day.
- Daydream about making love while doing the laundry, dishes, and so on.
- Call your spouse on your cordless phone and talk about your love life while you are doing a mundane chore like folding clothes or filing papers.
- Preset your florist's number (you do have a florist, don't you?) on your cellular phone. Regularly order a special surprise for your spouse while you travel to and from appointments.
- While checking your office e-mail, send your spouse an electronic love note.
- Leave an "I love you" voice mail.
- While getting ready for bed, pull out a candle and tune in some romantic music on the radio. It takes no time at all and may do wonders to put your otherwise unwilling spouse in the mood.

5. Guard Your Time

If you don't guard your time for each other, no one else will! When you are tempted to make a new time commit-

---

Post-My-Love Note

Post-it® notes are a favorite of mine. They are readily available and portable, and I always have them handy for emergencies or special surprises. Once when Claudia was at an appointment, I left the following note on her car: "Would the lovely, thin, trim, and relaxed owner of this car hurry to 8624 Dovefield Drive to meet your lover for a romantic rendezvous."

Dave

---

ment, first ask, "Will what I'm about to commit myself to bring us closer together or put distance in our relationship? What will I drop if I add something else?" One of the most helpful things we ever learned how to do was to say no (to others, not to each other!).

PROBLEM-SOLVING TIPS

*B*ut you don't understand my situation!" We have heard this comment so many times in our Marriage Alive seminars that we have come up with a list of ways to make time when there is none. These ideas require sacrifice, but the rewards of making time for each other are worth it.

- Take vacation time from work to spend time at home with your spouse. Rearrange your schedule to include a couple of hours at home alone without the kids.
- Reduce work hours. Evaluate why you are working so hard. Maybe you don't need more things but do need more time. We would rather spend half as much money on each other and twice as much time.
- Get a new job. This is extreme, but in some situations it's the smart thing to do.

Extreme Measures

I want to brag about a choice my husband made many years ago, though at the time I could have strangled him. Dave was working for a prominent Fortune 500 company that frequently required him to travel. His travel and work schedules were definitely taking their toll on our relationship, but I thought that was just what young "go-getting" junior executives did. Dave, however, had had enough. He loved spending time with his family and didn't think all his extra effort for the company was giving him much in return. He asked to be moved into a position that required less travel, and the company refused. So Dave immediately quit. Reacting shortsightedly, all I could do was worry about our next paycheck. But Dave had enough confidence in himself and in his decision for the both of us. It wasn't too long before Dave moved into a position that was much better suited to his temperament and gifts and was inherently more family friendly. That was one of the best decisions he ever made. While I can't recommend impetuously quitting a job (such extremism is rarely practical), I can say that making the decision to leave an ill-fitting career and boldly choosing family over that career was a smart move for us and may also be for you. It's all too easy to lose sight of what is truly important in life—spouses, children, friends—and sacrifice all that for an impersonal corporation or employer.

Claudia

- Take care of your health. Squeeze in naps, time-outs, and walks around the block. Failing to protect your health can become a liability to your love life!
- If money is tight, trade baby-sitting with another family. If you feel you don't know anyone well enough, make getting to know some folks a priority. You'd be surprised how many couples are in your same situation and would be thrilled at the suggestion to take turns baby-sitting. Introduce yourself to other parents at playgrounds, play groups, church nurseries,

and preschools. Some communities even have baby-sitting co-ops in which you have to be interviewed and approved to join but then you just trade services, not money, with other members.

• Hooray for the VCR! We love conducting informal surveys at the many conventions we have to attend. You can talk to so many people from all over the country in a short period of time. Recently our standard question has been, "And how do you find time for sex?" Many answers are amusing, from "Now, tell me—just what is sex?" to "We lock ourselves in the bathroom and tell our kids we have to fix the toilet." But perhaps one of the best tips came from our friend Greg, the father of two preschoolers: "It's easy—as soon as I hear the theme music from *Barney*, I become amorous! You don't think parents buy all those kiddy videos for the kids, do you? They're for us!" Don't

---

How I Find Time for Sex

When things get really crazy at our house, I call my best friend, who also has preschoolers. I say, "Red alert!" which lets her know I'm really desperate and need help! Then, if it's a "go," I call my husband and tell him when I'll pick him up at the office. Next I make a huge pot of spaghetti, a green salad, and butter two loaves of French bread. I set my table with paper plates for my friend's family and our kids. Then I pack the picnic basket, including a red-checked tablecloth, candles, and our favorite romantic CDs. I divide the spaghetti, salad, and bread, packing enough for two. As soon as my friend—my very good friend—arrives, I leave my kids at home with her and her children, hop in the car, pull out of our garage, drive to my husband's office, and pick him up. Then we head for an Italian romantic rendezvous at my very good friend's empty house! Next time I'm the very good friend!

Survey participant

---

feel guilty about plopping your kids in front of the TV every now and then. The benefit they will get from two refreshed and reconnected parents far outweighs any negatives of a short time spent staring at the television.

CREATIVITY IS STILL ALIVE!

We applaud all the parents in our survey who are courageously making time for sex. Creativity is alive and well. Read on.

"When we have time, we love to be creative. We're both very willing to try different things to make it interesting, and we're also not afraid to tell each other if something doesn't feel comfortable or good. Because of the lack of opportunity or time, we've been known to awaken in the middle of the night to have private time. That's desperate, I know, but in some ways it makes us feel a little adventurous, like in the old days."

This survey participant and her partner have learned how to make time to stay in touch and keep their love life going. Now it's your turn. Are you willing to make time for your marriage? Time for intimacy? Time for sex? Your marriage can be enriched, healthy, and growing—even in the midst of the hectic years of parenting.

> **Five Fantastic Magic Marriage Moments**
> 1. Take a shower together and wash each other's hair.
> 2. Write a love note on your steamy mirror.
> 3. Light a candle or oil lantern together.
> 4. Eat a banana split with two spoons.
> 5. Order two café au laits and look deeply into each other's eyes.

Eight

No Energy for Sex

I never thought I would ever lack energy for sex," Everett told Dave. "But after the second baby arrived, I entered a new realm of exhaustion. And now with a toddler and preschooler, things haven't gotten any better. Even on those rare occasions when we're both awake and interested, we'll never really relax—especially after what happened last week.

"Here's the scenario. Lately our love life has been on 'sleep mode.' But last Friday we had plans. Throughout the day we flirted with each other on the phone, at dinner, and as we got the kids in bed. Then at last it was our time. Assuming our kids were sound asleep, we were totally caught up in the romance of the moment, when a little voice at the side of our bed said, 'Daddy, can I ride next?' My wife was horrified and said she would not have sex again until the kids grew up and left home! Any advice?"

Stifling laughter, Dave responded, "Your heroic efforts to love each other and use energy wisely were really thwarted that time. But waiting until the kids grow up is not the answer! A simpler solution is to put a lock on your bedroom door—and use it!"

While the best-laid plans don't always work out, parents who want to be lovers must deal with the energy factor. A

The DINS Club

Do you find you're so exhausted that you are seldom in the mood for love? Are you a DINS (Double Income, No Sex) couple? Raising a family and making a living at the same time is not an easy assignment, but please don't give up on sex!

survey participant wrote, "Finding the time is easy—just go to bed. Finding the energy is the hard part!"

What can you do when you are just too tired to build a love life? We have three suggestions: (1) identify the "energy busters" that are robbing you of your enthusiasm for and interest in sex, (2) consider "energy boosters" that will make you generally feel better and improve your outlook on life, (3) find new "energy savers" that will help you have zest for romance, intimacy, and sex. Also, at the end of this chapter we offer tips from survey participants who, in the midst of parenting, are still finding energy for loving each other.

ENERGY BUSTERS

*W*hat are the energy busters in your life—those things that deplete you of physical or emotional strength and compromise your effectiveness as a parent and partner? Children were at the top of our list. Face it—you'd have more than enough to keep you busy if you did nothing but raise your children. Add careers, home maintenance, friends, and community and religious activities, and it's enough to keep anyone busy for several lifetimes. No wonder many parents complain of having no energy for sex. Why not take a good look at your life and identify your energy busters?

Too Many Commitments

If you're like the majority of partners who are parents, you have too much to do. OK, we know some of your pressing commitments carry over from your "before kids" days. And they may be really worthy efforts. Frankly, you might be hard pressed to get out of them, but too many outside commitments may be harmful to your family and your love life.

Take a hard look at how you spend your time and evaluate what activities you can easily eliminate from your schedule — usually those that don't affect anyone else. Then think about what additional activities you need to let go. As hard as it may be to disappoint a friend, relative, or coworker, you need to learn to say no to energy busters that take up your personal time, time with your family, and energy for your love life.

Time to Simplify

No matter how hard we try to compartmentalize our lives, a positive event or habit in one area of life affects all others, just as a negative event or habit can detrimentally impact seemingly unrelated areas. Our advice? Streamline and simplify life in the parenting years so your energies are going only to those things that positively affect your family and your love life.

Dave and Claudia

What to Keep? What to Let Go?

Identifying what to let go is tough, because discretionary activities include those things that may seem important but do not immediately or directly contribute to your family or marriage. For instance, an activity like volunteering at a homeless shelter may indeed benefit your family as you model appropriate citizen behavior. But if volunteering

Three Questions to Help You Make Hard Choices

Too many commitments? These three questions will help you weed them out.

1. *Is this activity essential?* Would the sky fall in if you didn't do this? For instance, you have to earn a living, care for your children, sleep, and eat.

2. *Is this activity really important?* Does it help you to be a better spouse or parent? For us a healthy diet, exercise, devotions and prayer, and regular dates enhance our relationship with each other and with our children. If you are a young parent, taking your children to play group can be a very important activity!

3. *Is this activity discretionary?* Is it optional, simply your choice, something you like to do? This might include civic and community activities or more personal things like watching television, staying after work on Friday evenings for social hour, or golfing.

is at the expense of your marriage relationship or your family's health, it is completely discretionary and might need to be dropped. Think about it, decide what's best for you, then act on your decision.

No Time for Me

"Sex life—what's a sex life?" one survey participant wrote. "Oh yes, that's what we had *before* we had kids. It's no big surprise that our sex life is dormant. I invest my time and energy meeting everyone else's needs. There's no time left over for just me. I feel as if I am losing myself."

Everyone needs some personal time—time to nurture themselves. What are those things that help you regroup and restore your energy reserve? Some may seem frivolous, but times of personal refreshment and renewal need to be built into your schedule and guarded as fiercely as any other important activity.

No Exercise and Poor Diet

Nothing zaps energy as much as a high-fat, high-sugar diet with little or no exercise. Understanding how diet and exercise affect energy levels should encourage you to make needed changes in your lifestyle. Simply modifying your diet and increasing your exercise can help energize your love life. We'll look at this area in greater depth as we discuss specific ways to improve your energy level.

No Help or Unequal Division of Labor

Are you tired all the time, while your partner manages to gets a full night's sleep and plenty of recreation and relaxation? Surprisingly, this is a common scenario among young parents. We are all familiar with the stereotype—the wife who just assumes she should single-handedly do the evening's dishes, give the kids a bath, pick up the house, and do the grocery shopping, all while her husband is watching the news after his "long" day at work. Hogwash! Both partners should share the load. If both partners are giving equal effort and if the husband is finished at 7:00 P.M., while the wife has two hours to go before she finishes, the husband should offer

---

How We Survived

When our boys were young, we had a general routine—naps or quiet times after lunch, dinner around 6:30 P.M., and bedtime rituals that included bath time, stories, prayers, cuddles, and so on. Our schedule wasn't rigid and some days we completely scrapped it. But having a basic plan for each day helped us to pace ourselves and sometimes still have energy for each other after the children were snug in their beds.

Claudia

---

to chip in—or vice versa! Sharing responsibility and working together ensures that no one partner has to carry too
heavy a burden and that no misplaced resentment develops.

No Structure

Another energy buster is lack of structure. We are spontaneous and like surprises and flexibility. But we never
would have survived our parenting years if we had not
imposed some structure on our schedules. Simply responding to crises instead of proactively balancing responsibilities is a sure recipe for disaster and lack of energy.

Some like more structure than others, but all families
need some structure.

ENERGY BOOSTERS

*W*hen you're tired and lack stamina, it's hard to imagine
having a fun, energized love life. But taking simple
steps to increase your energy level will help you handle your
responsibilities and reserve some energy for loving each
other. You don't have to wait for the kids to grow up to find
energy for sex! Here are some ways you can boost your
energy right now.

Take Care of <u>You</u>!

We've said it before and we'll say it again: You must be
good to yourself. You must nurture your mind, body, and
spirit before you can be good to others. Resist feeling guilty
about the time you take away from your children to take
care of yourself. You aren't being selfish. You are modeling
healthy living, and this will serve your children well over
their lifetimes. Consider these four commonsense tips for
taking care of you.

Stay Intellectually Stimulated

Staying sharp mentally is particularly important if you are a parent staying at home with the kids. Keeping your mind active will keep you in touch with the world outside your home, make you a better parent and a better conversationalist with your spouse, and improve your self-esteem. One survey participant wrote, "I realized I needed to find ways to stay intellectually stimulated when one day I talked to a telemarketing person for fifteen minutes—I just wanted to talk to another adult!"

Get Regular Exercise

Fifteen to thirty minutes of aerobic exercise three times each week is the current recommendation to maintain physical health. Each day, we try to take a brisk walk—which means we actually "fitness walk" three or four times a week. However much time you can carve out, make exercise a

---

Intellectual Stimulators

You can have kids and intellectual stimulation too. You just have to look for it. And you have to pick and choose what is realistic for you. Consider these stimulators.

- Listen to news and interviews on talk radio.
- Read a weekly news magazine.
- Keep a journal.
- Call one adult friend each day.
- Attend a monthly lecture.
- Join a monthly book club or a chat line that focuses on an interesting subject.
- On your own begin to learn French, German, Spanish, or the foreign language of your choice.

**Shortcut Workouts for
Busy Parents**

Don't have time to stay in shape? Try some of these suggestions.

• Do standing push-ups against the kitchen counter.
• Jump rope.
• Walk and talk while pushing the stroller.
• Lie on your back and lift your baby instead of weights.
• Go up and down the stairs twice.

habit. Even five minutes of daily stretches can raise your level of physical fitness—which increases your energy for loving your partner. If you make exercise a set part of your schedule, you will be more likely to do it.

Watch Your Diet

Eating healthy will boost your energy level. Cutting out high-fat foods will make you feel less sluggish. High-energy foods such as pasta, fruit, and yogurt can support you throughout the day. To get a better handle on ways to maximize your energy through eating, read a book about nutrition. If you have a hard time changing the way you eat, adding high-energy vitamins to your diet may be just the thing you need. Of course, you should check with your doctor first and then check out all the combination packs and strange-sounding vitamins that promise unending energy for life and loving. We wonder if they have a "parents-of-toddlers" mix. That would sell!

Five Healthy Snacks

1. fruits such as apples, oranges, and bananas
2. nonfat yogurt
3. raw vegetables with non- or low-fat dip
4. raisins and nuts
5. tall glass of ice water with a slice of lime or lemon

Time for Me

When our boys were young, one important thing I did for myself was having a daily time for devotions and reflection. In a notebook I journaled my thoughts and concerns and recorded specific prayers. This personal time of reflection helped me connect with my heavenly Father and renew my spirit. I was able to put life in perspective, and as a result I was a much nicer mom and mate! Of course, I had to be flexible to find this time, and it didn't happen every day, but because I intentionally sought it, I found it more often than not.

Claudia

Take Time for Yourself

It's not always easy, but carve out some personal time to nurture yourself. This may mean taking fifteen minutes after the kids go to bed to sit quietly in a darkened room and unwind. Or it may mean getting away from the house and kids for a quiet cup of coffee. If at all possible you should have some of this time daily. But build it in when you can. Again, to give your best to your spouse and your kids and to be a great lover, you need to feel at peace with yourself.

Restructure Your Life

Restructuring your life sounds like a big task, doesn't it? We've touched on some of these points before, but we want to reiterate how something as simple as getting kids in bed fifteen minutes earlier or keeping your baby-sitter "on call" for Friday nights can provide you with a needed break from parenting and increase your enthusiasm for loving. Consider three areas that may need restructuring.

Household Chores

Get the kids to help. You'd be surprised at how much toddlers enjoy helping. Two-year-old Henry loves to help his
mommy mop the floor. She sprays wood soap in a small area,
and he scrubs his heart out on all of the "bubbles." Choose
age-appropriate tasks, of course, but teaching your children
to pitch in is an important part of functioning in today's world.

Children Helper Tips

Young children can be helpers, especially if you lower your
standards! Here are some suggestions for age-appropriate help.

Ages Two to Four
> Pick up toys
> Clean up dropped food
> Help mommy dust—especially the floor
> Make simple decisions such as choosing between two
>   foods
> Simple hygiene—brush teeth, wash and dry hands

Ages Four to Six
> Set the table
> Put groceries away
> Feed pets
> Dust the furniture
> Make bed

Elementary School
> Choose clothes for the day
> Be a kitchen helper
> Make simple school lunch
> Water plants
> Clean room
> Take phone messages
> Begin to learn how to use washer and dryer[1]

For a guide to knowing what your children are and are not capable of doing, we recommend the excellent book *Children Who Do Too Little* by Patricia Sprinkle (Zondervan, 1996).

Naps and Bedtime

Make this time count for your good. Boycott soap operas and sitcoms. Instead of collapsing on the couch in front of the television, do something that is truly relaxing and nurturing, like taking a bath or having a cup of tea and reading a good book. Or make the time superproductive. Blitz it. You'll be amazed at how much you can accomplish in just one hour without the constant interruptions of small children. And on those days when you're exhausted, take a nap yourself.

> **Five Ways to Say No (but Not to Sex!)**
> 1. "I've done it in the past, and I'll do it in the future, but I can't do it at the present."
> 2. "I'm sorry. I'll just have to pass this time."
> 3. "I'm flattered you asked, but I'll have to say no this time."
> 4. "No."
> 5. Five-star no: "No, I have no desire, time, or energy. It's simply impossible. No!"

Obligations

Keep outside commitments to a minimum, learn to say no, and enlist help when you need it. If you really have to stay late at work three nights each week, consider going in late to work one day a week and spending a leisurely breakfast with your preschoolers.

~

The key to restructuring your life is to be honest about your needs and priorities and then be creative in how you approach your particular time constraints.

Enlist Help

No one person can do it all! Even two parents working together may have difficulty getting everything done. Look for folks who can give you a break, lend a helping hand, or just provide a listening ear when you're at the end of your rope. Help is out there; you just have to find it!

ENERGY SAVERS

*L*ittle things mean a lot" is the message we keep getting from the parents we meet. Most of them have offered creative, simple suggestions for conserving energy.

- "Turn off the television and go to bed earlier."
- "Don't answer the phone after 9:00 P.M."

Ways Creative Parents Enlist Help

- "I get together with some other moms, and we share chores like going to the grocery store. One parent can watch the children while the other shops."
- "When it gets crazy, I fax my grocery list to a full-service store and later pick up my groceries. This has been a real time and energy saver for me."
- "I use a twelve-year-old neighborhood girl as my 'mother's helper.' She entertains my preschoolers while I clean the house or even take a nap. Although she may not be the most reliable sitter in the world—I don't leave her completely alone with my kids—she is affordable and has endless energy to throw the ball or paint and color with my kids. And in the future she will be a great sitter—all trained and familiar to my kids!"
- "I joined a co-op play group. This gives me two or three hours of free time each week."
- "I trade baby-sitting with other parents."

- "Shower together."
- "Read books together."
- "Enforce kids' bedtime."
- "Take advantage of visiting grandparents."
- "Learn how to massage."
- "Daily pray for wisdom and discernment with priorities."
- "Take Saturday and Sunday 'naps.'"
- "Save a few special toys to bring out only when you need a few minutes of quiet time."
- "Divide and conquer evening chores."

ENERGY FOR LOVING

*O*f course, our goal in this book is to help you build your love life. The suggestions in this chapter are designed to generally improve your energy and specifically help you have energy left over for loving. Especially when you have young children, time and energy will always be a precious commodity. Just remember to cherish the moments you have and make the most of every day.

Tips for Having a Love Life When Energy Is Low

We conclude this chapter with some of the best tips from our survey participants for keeping intimacy and romance alive when the energy level is registering "low."

- "On Sunday afternoons we tell the kids Mom and Dad need a nap, and we are not to be disturbed unless the house is on fire. We always invite them to take a nap, too. They are horrified at the thought and disappear."
- "Often we awaken before the alarm goes off, and that's the time when we are physically fresh."

- "Sundays after church we come home and put on a special video for the kids and tell them not to disturb us because we'll be very busy 'cleaning our room.'"
- "We swap kids overnight with our good friends."
- "I worked to get our kids' nap schedules down to where they're sleeping when my husband comes home for lunch."
- "Sometimes we get a baby-sitter just for a couple of hours and stay home together instead of going out."
- "Put on a video for the kids and lock the door."
- "We make appointments with each other."
- "Plan ahead. Agree to make love at least once a week and keep track."
- "Meet at home for a date while the kids are at school. You could even take a day off work."
- "Find a sitter who will let you take the kids to her house. Then go home for romance and fun."
- "Recently we took a blanket outside under the trees at 1:30 A.M."
- "Don't get stuck in a rut. Any time of day or night needs to remain as an option."
- "Have several minutes of together time in your candlelit bedroom before retiring."
- "Take advantage of the moments. Don't wait for everything to be perfect."
- "Saturday morning cartoons are awesome!"

Nine

~

"Mommy and Daddy Are Busy Now"

I don't know how it came to this!" Ellie sobbed. "Where did we go wrong?" Her husband of eighteen years had, without any warning, packed up his bags and moved out. "In the beginning of our marriage we had such a good relationship. Our sex life was great. As a matter of fact, life for us was so good, we weren't sure we wanted to have kids. But after a number of years my biological clock was running out, and we made that big decision to start a family. Within a year Becky was born, and two years later Charlie came along. Frankly, we didn't know what hit us!

"With our first baby we were both nervous and overprotective. She was high-strung, which didn't help at all. I began lying down with her and nursing her to sleep. Sometimes I was so tired, I didn't put her in her crib. (It's not easy having children in your late thirties.) Frank, seeing us asleep and not wanting to wake us, would sleep in the guest room or on the couch. Unfortunately, this became a pattern, one that continued when Charlie was born.

"Now our children are six and eight. In addition to all their demands during the day, they still expect me to lie down with them when they go to bed. I'm basically a morning person, and after the hassle of getting them settled at night, there's nothing left of me to give to Frank. Our intimate times together over the last several years have been rather sketchy. I should have seen it coming. It's been weeks—no, to be honest, it's been months since we've had sex."

As Ellie continued, she told us how her parenting role had overshadowed her role as a partner. "There were no boundaries between being a partner and being a parent. I was an on-call mom twenty-four hours a day. That didn't leave much time for Frank." But Frank's not off the hook. He also took a passive role in maintaining their marriage and their love life. He chose to focus most of his time and energy in building his company and getting ahead. "You do that," he later told us, "by working hard and working long hours. And with Ellie so committed to the children, there wasn't that much to come home for. Finally I realized we didn't even know each other anymore. We didn't have a personal relationship—much less a sexual one. So I thought it was time to get on with my life. I'm not getting any younger, you know."

What's wrong with this picture? How can a couple have a great love life and relationship the first ten years of their marriage and lose it after children come along? What could they have done differently? What message were they passing on to their kids about the sanctity of marriage? Is there some way they could have taught their children to respect their marriage? Is it possible to be good parents and build a good marriage at the same time? Our answer to the last two questions is emphatically yes!

But you must put your marriage first. Putting kids first can damage your marriage and is a poor example for your children. While you love your children dearly, you need to teach them to respect your marriage and your need for time alone together. This will help your children be other-centered and recognize the importance of the marriage relationship.

TIPS FOR TEACHING MARITAL RESPECT

One of the best things you can do for your kids is to love each other. Your children will feel a special security when your marriage relationship is strong, loving, and healthy. So when you take time to love each other, you can be confident that you are adding to your children's sense of security.

Our boys would roll their eyes and say, "Mom and Dad are at it again!" when they caught us hugging and kissing. But that was life at the Arps'. We were determined to be affectionate with each other and to protect our "just for two" times. Never did we feel guilty when we locked our bedroom door! So over the years, through the school of experience we found four key ways to teach our children to respect our relationship and our need for time alone: (1) we created our own private space, (2) we cultivated our own private times, (3) we let our children see us being affectionate and let them ask questions about our marriage relationship, (4) we built friendships with other adults.

Let's look closer as each of the ways we tried to teach our children to respect our marriage.

Create Your Own Private Space

A great sex life is dependent upon having a place to be intimate. With no privacy there is little romance. One wife told us, "Our house is great for our kids, the pets, our friends, company, but it doesn't work so well for us. We have no privacy! Our kids wander in and out of our bedroom like it is Grand Central Station!"

"It's time to railroad them out of your bedroom," we responded. "And close the door! It's critical that you have your own private space in your home. And we do mean physical space—whether it's your bedroom, study, or even the master bathroom. It's where children must have special permission to enter. Your private space can be a sanctuary where you can be alone and focus on loving each other. It serves as your refuge from the overwhelming needs and chaos of family life."

If you have toddlers who need close supervision or if you live in an apartment in which the bedroom doubles as a play space, this may be unrealistic. But once your children don't need to be with you in your bedroom, make your room off-limits. Never make your bedroom the "family room." Teach your children to knock before entering. (Children can learn to do this at a very early age.) Resist using your bedroom as an office. It is not the place for your sewing machine or computer. It can become the place where you nurture each other and occasionally find solitude.

How to Have a Five-Star Bedroom
on a One-Star Budget

- Add candles, candles, and more candles. Don't forget scented ones!
- Music enhances romance. Put your CD player or audiotape recorder in your bedroom. Even an inexpensive radio will work—there are a number of great classical and easy-listening stations that will help create a romantic atmosphere.
- Add a dimmer switch to your overhead light.
- A grouping of pillows is inexpensive and adds a wonderful ambiance.
- Frame pictures of the two of you.
- Matching bathrobes will complete your makeover!

Child Space

We learned over the years that if we wanted our children to respect our space, we also had to respect theirs. From the time they were very young we did what we could to provide each child with his own space. Sometimes this necessitated being creative with room dividers, curtains, and bookcases, but it was important to us—and to them. As our children grew, we learned to knock on their door and respected their right to create an environment comfortable to them (within certain parameters, of course).

Dave and Claudia

Claim your space. Add whatever touches you need to create a loving and romantic atmosphere. Toys are out and candles are in! If your finances are limited and you have to choose, invest in your relationship by upgrading your bedroom first before remodeling a living room or dining room.

We have created sitting areas, even in small bedrooms, where we could retreat from our teenagers and read or talk in quiet. A grouping of wedding pictures reminds us of the commitment we made long ago to each other.

When we built our condo, we treated ourselves and created a dream bathroom including dual showerheads and Jacuzzi tub. A chandelier for candles, not electric lights, graces the space above the tub. And a basket of fresh towels, bath salts, and body oils completes the effect. Now we understand why so many of the new homes have such spacious master bathrooms!

Even if you have small children, you can enjoy these private spaces. Having a nursery monitor or several monitors (turned down low but loud enough to hear a crisis) will enable you to close the bedroom or bathroom door and still make sure no one is waking up or getting into a fight.

Cultivate Your Own Private Times

Having a romantic place is a start, but you need to use it! We suggest two types of private times: *adult time,* when your kids may still be around but you aren't focusing on them, and *alone time,* when your children are safely in bed or otherwise occupied in their own rooms, and you can concentrate on loving.

Adult Time

As soon as children are old enough to understand, teach them about adult time. Start with short blocks of time when your child must find something other than you to occupy his or her attention. The sooner your children learn to entertain themselves, the easier it will be to increase your adult times. Even if you can't escape to your hideaway, you can still sit on the sofa, talking and cuddling.

Alone Time

Finding alone time is often harder but just as important. The best step you can take toward having time alone with your mate is to set and enforce a bedtime for your children. Did we hear you groan? Of course, this time will change, depending upon the age of your child, and you can count on occasional disruptions to your routine. But knowing that your children will be in their rooms after a certain time allows you to plan special moments and increase your anticipation of the bedtime hour.

After spending most of her life trying to be everything to everyone and finally facing clinical depression, Jan Dravecky, wife of former baseball star, Dave Dravecky, changed her priorities. She says, "Whereas I used to stay up to finish my work regardless of how tired I was, I now make sure I'm in my bedroom by 9:00 p.m. . . . I've made it a rule

---

Bedtime Sanity Tip

If your children already have a bedtime routine but their bedtime
is too late and you're exhausted by the time they're asleep, change
their bedtime ritual and move everything up thirty to sixty minutes.
Your children may not go right to sleep (and count on them complaining!), but at least they can stay in their rooms. Older children
can read, listen to tapes, or do other quiet activities. At first you
may feel that you're not being responsive to your children or that
this scheduling doesn't suit your parenting style, but remember that
you are fighting for your marriage here. And if the only way you
can manage to find some private time for loving (and we don't
mean half-asleep sex) is to enforce a bedtime, do it. Your marriage
will benefit, and ultimately your children will benefit, too.

---

of thumb that once I've cooked supper, my housework and
ministry work is done for the day."[1] Whether or not her
schedule is practical for you is something only you can
decide. We do want to encourage you again, however, to prioritize your responsibilities and schedule times for loving.

Be Openly Affectionate

Children need to realize that the relationship between
their mother and father is distinct and not dependent on
them. It's helpful for them to learn that they are *not* the center of your universe and that your marriage existed before
they arrived and will continue after they leave. As we previously emphasized, they will feel more secure and loved as
you model a healthy marriage. Caring for your marriage will
give them a reference for their future romantic relationships.

The level of affection you're comfortable displaying will
vary from couple to couple, but remember, it's healthy for
your children to overhear loving remarks and to see you
hold hands, cuddle on the couch, or kiss. We didn't hide

our love notes left on the kitchen counter or office door, and while we didn't discuss our love life with our children, they were aware of why we liked to go away for the week-end or have time alone in our bedroom. Our openness helped our sons learn practical ways couples can express love to one another. We are thrilled when we see them—now all married—leaving their own notes, sending flowers, or taking special weekends away.

Author Bob Barnes gives a suggestion for dealing with older children and bedtimes. He and his wife, Rosemary, wanted to have the family room (which included a fireplace) to themselves one evening. He told their teenage daughter that she didn't have to go to sleep but she had to be in her room for the night by 9:00. She balked and said, "What will happen if I come into the family room after 9:00?" Her dad replied, "You'll see two naked bodies in front of the fireplace!" Needless to say, Bob and Rosemary were not disturbed that evening.[2]

Perhaps that reply was a little shocking, but his point is well made. Sometimes finding alone time can be tougher when children are older. Hear us: You are not bad parents when you insist on alone time. You are teaching your children a lesson that will strengthen their own marriages. (Though, if you're like us, you may be more comfortable with a lock on the door!)

Tested Child Entertainers

For those times when you have guests or you want adult time, consider the following:

- Bring out a special toy that they like but don't often get to play with.
- Give them a new book they are eager to read.
- Let them invite a friend to sleep over at your house.
- Let them watch a special video.

"Just You and Me" Times

We found that when we spent private time with each of our children, they were more willing to accept that Mom and Dad needed time alone together or with friends. At an early age we initiated "just you and me" times—time alone for one parent and one child to talk, kick the soccer ball, or go to the library or out for hot chocolate. Our "just you and me" times were not always large blocks of time. Sometimes as little as ten or fifteen minutes in the kitchen with cookies and milk was sufficient to have that "just two" feeling.

This tradition helped greatly when we wanted to be alone or with our adult friends.

Dave and Claudia

Build Friendships with Other Adults

Talking about cultivating adult friendships may seem odd in a book about improving your love life, but it reinforces the notion that there is an adult world and a child's world. And while both worlds often intersect, they are distinct and important components in a healthy life. Through your interaction with other grown-ups you'll be providing your children with models of marriage relationships and adult friendships that broaden their frame of reference. Your kids will also see that you two aren't the only adults in the world who like to hold hands or cuddle, thereby making you more like everyone else and less creepy.

The younger your children are when they see you building friendships with other adults the better, because they will accept this as a normal part of their life. If, however, you find that your kids fight to be the center of attention when you have company, changing their behavior may take some persistence. It's worth the effort, and when your kids

finally get the hang of it, you can have large blocks of uninterrupted time with your adult friends.

THE FOUR Rs

*T*eaching children to respect your marriage might not be
the easiest thing in the world to do, but you will be so
glad you did it. As some final encouragement, we want to
share with you the four principles we stress in our parenting seminars. These basic, tried-and-true principles apply
to all stages of your children's lives. They will give you confidence as you seek to be intentional and thoughtful as a
parent and will help you with whatever parenting dilemma
you face.

Regroup

Regrouping and evaluating the status of your children's
development and your parenting approach is an essential
component of a healthy family. Children go through different developmental stages, necessitating changes in the ways
you relate to them. Some stages are more difficult than others and will require you to work together as parents more
than others. We encourage all parents to do some reading
about the stages of child development and then plan regular
times as a couple to discuss each child's growth and needs.

Relate

The key to a healthy child and happy family is the quality of the parent-child relationship. Instead of overempha-
sizing minor issues like how your child dresses or whether
they are in enough extracurricular activities to get into college, spend time building your relationship with your children, demonstrating your love and commitment to them.

The security they have in their relationship with you will provide them with the internal resources they need to face the challenges of today's world far more than how well their outfits coordinate or how tidy their room is.

Release

Your kids will only be with you for a short time. You need to have the perspective that parenting is a temporary job with the goal of developing a person who can successfully live independently of you. So, as appropriate for their age, encourage your children to take responsibility for their own decisions and lives, and spend more time solidifying the relationships that will last for a lifetime.

Relax

Parenting should be a pleasure. Your marriage should be a pleasure. So give yourself permission to take time to have fun with your kids and with your mate. Take time to laugh. Be unpredictable. Pace yourself. And periodically take a short break so you can come back to your home refreshed and better able to meet the challenges of parenting and marriage.

～

Your children can enrich your marriage, and your marriage can enrich your children. The two can work together when you teach your children to respect your marriage. Now that the kids are occupied, it's time for you to have some fun and to schedule sex! That will be our goal in the next chapter.

Ten

~

Sex on a Schedule

"Can you help? We have a problem with intimacy," a female reader writes. "We dated two years before we were married, and as difficult as it was, we saved sex for marriage. Our honeymoon was wonderful, and we had a great love life during the first part of our marriage—the part before kids! We were spontaneous and romance was alive. But since kids—we have three preschoolers, ages one, two, and three—we have a problem even being sexually intimate.

"Frankly, after three children climb on me all day, I just don't want to be touched. I want my 'personal space' back. I end up making myself be intimate because I know my husband wants sex. My husband knows this, and it doesn't help our love life at all. Our sex is also very routine and mechanical. In addition to this, I have put on forty extra pounds since my first pregnancy, and this affects my self-image. So besides wanting my body left untouched, lack of arousal, boredom, and my weight problem, I'm usually exhausted after taking care of my three toddlers all day. Do you have any suggestions for this most hopeless sexual relationship? How can we get back a little of the spontaneity and romance and reignite a faltering love life?"

While this reader's situation is desperate, we wouldn't classify it as hopeless. In the deep, dark recesses of her mind are memories of a brighter day and an enjoyable love life.

But if she is expecting spontaneity and romance to automatically reappear, she is dreaming. Revitalizing a flat love life is hard work, but step by step, sexual intimacy and vitality can be renewed.

Maybe your situation isn't so desperate. Some people bounce into the parenting years without missing a beat! For instance, another reader, in response to our article "Love Life for the Very Married Parent" in *Christian Parenting Today* wrote, "My husband and I just celebrated our fifth wedding anniversary. We have a three-and-a-half-year-old daughter and another child on the way. The scenarios described in your article are foreign to us; we have had no problems maintaining a good marriage and sex life after the arrival of children.

"We put our daughter to bed at 8:00 P.M. each night. My husband and I do not retire until 10:00 P.M. This leaves us two hours of peace, quiet, and togetherness each night. We have taught our daughter right from the beginning that once she is in bed, she stays in bed. She is strong-willed, but we have no trouble maintaining peace at bedtime, because this routine is strictly enforced and she has learned that it does no good to fight it. So my husband and I can look forward to the last two hours of each day. We have time to sit and talk, enjoy our hot tub, watch a movie together, or be romantic."

We considered asking the second reader to write to the first reader but decided they live on different planets. Where would you place your own experience? If you are like most parents, you probably fall somewhere in between. Most of us experience some frustration and need encouragement.

Over the years as we lived through the many stages of active parenting, we discovered that our sexual relationship progressed or regressed in direct proportion to the attention we gave it. At all stages we need to build an intentional love life—yes, even now we need to schedule sex! It has worked for us and it can work for you too! You can have kids and a love life too!

In this chapter we will tell you how to revitalize your love life by integrating loving habits into family life and how to overcome the barriers of ever-present kids. We will share how we overcame the inertia of ignorance and became informed and educated lovers—while parenting our kids! Then we will challenge you to take the initiative—you can add spontaneity and romance to your love life by scheduling sex.

REIGNITING THE SPARK

Have cotton nightshirts replaced sexy lingerie? Have the sounds of Madeline and Barney videos replaced the sounds of your favorite romantic CDs? Are romance, intimacy, and sex vague memories? Then you can identify with most young parents.

In a recent *Ladies Home Journal* poll, fifteen hundred baby boomers in their thirties and forties were asked, "What is your idea of a perfect evening?" Would you believe that only 7 percent responded, "Romance and making love!" Eighty-nine percent said they were stressed out some or most of the time![1]

One reason our love life takes a nosedive after kids arrive is exhaustion and sleep deprivation. You'd like to reignite the spark, but you just don't know where to start.

The Spanish poet Antonio Machado wrote, "I thought the fire was out in my fireplace. I stirred the ashes, and I

Tips for Renewing the Spark

- Talk about your desires and expectations (review chapters 4, 5, and 6).
- Really listen to each other!
- Spend some time alone. Pamper yourself and then you will be more inclined to pamper each other!
- Make a special date when, as a couple, you can be totally alone.
- Be adventuresome. Be willing to experiment.
- Learn to pace yourself.
- Schedule sex!

burned my hands." We are convinced that you can experience the same phenomenon in your love life when you intentionally seek to reignite the spark. But you need to be realistic.

Leslie Schover, staff psychologist at the Cleveland Clinic Foundation's Center for Sexual Function, says this: "We expect people will fall in love, be each other's best friends for life, and have passionate sex every night. But this ideal for marriage is impossible. It's best to think more about quality than quantity."[2]

So to reignite that spark, think quality, not quantity. And be practical! One of the best things you can do to rekindle your love life is to take a nap! We actually have advised parents to have a sleep date! Get away for twenty-four hours, but spend the first part of it sleeping! Only then is it time to fan that flickering spark.

NURTURING INTIMACY WHILE THE KIDS ARE UNDERFOOT

How can you integrate loving habits into your family life? We've already said it's healthy for your kids to see you flirt with each other. Hugs and kisses and loving gestures help to relieve fears that mom and dad are going to get a divorce. Unfortunately, this is one of the major fears of children today. So when your children roll their eyes as you give their mommy or daddy a kiss, just remember that they need this as much as you do!

So how do you nurture intimacy when the kids are underfoot? Here are some suggestions from our survey participants.

- "We touch a lot. We hug, kiss, hold hands, sit next to each other."
- "Court your mate each day in some special way. This definitely boosts our interest, and we're good models for our children!"
- "Laugh a lot."
- "Have children help plan your date. They pick the baby-sitter and where you go (within reason—Chuck E. Cheese doesn't cut it!)."
- "Put your mate first and the children second."
- "A weekly date is a must, even if it's just to run errands. Our children know that this is 'mommy and daddy' time."
- "Don't be afraid to show your children how much you love your spouse. Do lots of hugging and kissing and snuggling in front of them. Let them see that it's healthy to do so. Make dates with your spouse. Your kids need the break, too!"
- "Let parents' bedroom be 'restricted zone.' No entry without permission!"
- "We don't worry about the kids knowing what we are doing. We explain to the kids that we need time for us to develop as a couple in order to be better parents. After several of their friends' parents have divorced, this really makes an impact."
- "We remember that when we love each other, we are being good role models to our children."

- "Let your kids know you love them with all your heart but that they can't consume all of your time and energy. Sometimes Mom and Dad need to talk, and they shouldn't interrupt."

BECOMING EDUCATED LOVERS

*H*ave you heard the old joke about the couple making love? They were still learning how to please each other and trying to use communication skills—as in talking to each other about their lovemaking. The wife was beginning to feel amorous and wanted to help direct her husband's gentle caresses, so as he said, "I love you! I love you!" she responded, "Lower! Lower!"—to which he replied in a deeper voice, "I love you! I love you!"

Though that particular scenario is funny, maybe you also have a lot to learn. Yet do you draw back because of ignorance, inhibitions, past history, or attitudes gleaned from your childhood and brought into marriage? Don't assume you worked through all these before you had children.

Whatever your sexual education background—whether you were uneducated or well-educated—you still have much potential for learning and growing together in sexual intimacy. You need to be reminded of what you already know. But—especially as parents—you also need a designated time and place to further your sexual education!

Your Private Sex School

We've already shared that when our boys were quite young, we designated Monday mornings as our time. With a flexible work schedule (we could both take Monday mornings off), Mom's Day Out, kindergarten, and school, we were able to schedule two hours alone for each Monday morning. For those two hours we did not answer the door and our phone was off the hook (or curious Claudia would have answered it!). Basically, we were unavailable to anything or anybody, so we were *totally* available to each other! This was our time to learn how to be great lovers. Years later we are reaping benefits from our Monday mornings.

While Monday mornings eventually ended, over the years we have continued to schedule time for sex education. Becoming great lovers is an acquired skill. While there may be some people who are naturals, we have always classified ourselves as learners. The knowledge we have today about sex was not gained because we're naturally great lovers. Instead we're great lovers because of what we know and have learned about sex!

What motivated us to develop sexual expertise? Dave's strong sex drive and Claudia's adventuresome spirit and thirst for knowledge certainly were factors. Plus, working for many years helping marriages, leading seminars, and writing books has enriched our love life.

When we were writing our first book, *Ten Dates for Mates* (now revised and titled *10 Great Dates to Revitalize Your Marriage* [Zondervan, 1997]), we read every book we could get our hands on. We talked to every couple who

---

For Husbands Only

You can increase your wife's pleasure. Women can learn how to be orgasmic and even multiorgasmic. (For more on this topic, we recommend *The Gift of Sex* by Clifford and Joyce Penner [Word, 1981]). While you might be thinking, "That's not fair!" stop and consider the advantages for you.

- It raises the stakes for your wife.
- It creates more interest on her part.
- It benefits you and doubles your pleasure.

Dave

would talk to us. (Few couples would talk about sex.) After we researched a subject, we experimented. Some things we liked, so we repeated them. Some things we didn't like. (Chocolate syrup is messy, while whipped cream is great!) Here are some of the things we learned.

Your Mate's Pleasure Will Double Yours!

Learn what brings pleasure to your spouse. The sexual experience is like two unique musical instruments harmonizing together, playing a beautiful song that both enjoy. The instruments are different and respond in different ways to touch and stimulation. At times one instrument takes the lead in the song, and vice versa. Both do not have to sound the high note at the same time! Both instruments seek to complement the other. So in lovemaking discover how to please each other in different ways. Let each lead from time to time. You can find wonderful harmony!

For Wives Only

Don't let sex become another job or responsibility. The rewards are worth all the time and effort it will take to learn how to respond to your husband. Don't bypass the emotions—even if you are not able or don't want to reach a climax each time you have a loving interlude, stay connected emotionally. Be transparent and don't ever fake a response! Give yourself permission to be a sexual person, to have feelings, to surrender to your husband, to embrace sexual adventure!

Claudia

Understanding Male and Female Differences Will Enhance Your Love Life

In the initial stage of lovemaking, the wife needs gentle caresses and stimulation. She doesn't respond to a drumroll but rather to the quiet strings of a classical guitar. She may actually prefer to reach her high notes before the husband penetrates and reaches his. The husband can facilitate this in many specific ways to make sure she enjoys the experience. After penetration, if the husband continues to stimulate his wife with his loving touch, she may even climax again! In a lovely musical piece, there are many crescendos. Learn how to create your own musical score.

Learn to Please Each Other

"Our love life can be playful, serious, or very intense, depending on the mood. While I have a much greater desire for sexual variety and exploration (my wife is comfortable with a pretty set routine for sex), we have learned to pleasure each other. The greatest stress is in keeping our sex life fun and from becoming routine."

Survey participant

Keep Learning All You Can and Become Familiar with the Stages of Lovemaking

There is always something new to learn! Read about and study the stages of lovemaking. For some couples, just knowing to use KY Jelly for extra lubrication makes a tremendous difference. But remember, what the books say is not always

Tips for Exploring and Experimenting

We suggest adopting the following guidelines:

- Whatever we try must be mutually acceptable.
- We will always seek to please the other.
- We must have privacy whenever we are exploring and experimenting.
- We will talk openly about whatever we are trying. (Otherwise it's easy to misunderstand each other.)

Dave and Claudia

Steps for Revitalizing Your Love Life

1. *Talk and review.* Talk about your needs and expectations, review the love à la carte menu (chapter 6), and work on increasing your sexual vocabulary.
2. *Explore.* Read, learn, and practice! Discover what feels good, learn about each other's body, and relearn the mechanics of sex.
3. *Do the unexpected.* Be creative and surprise each other.
4. *Schedule sex!* It's time to pull out that calendar.

true for everyone. Some wives need lubricant all the time. You need to express to each other when you are "ready."

Your most important sex organ is your brain! So talk, talk, talk! Educate each other. Sex is a trust relationship. It is opening yourself up to another person in the most intimate way. Tell your lover what you like and what you don't like. Be willing to experiment.

Set Your Own Guidelines for Exploring and Experimenting

If you agree beforehand on what is acceptable to both of you, you can relax and enjoy exploring and experimenting. But you need to take the time to explore and experiment— especially if you want to keep your love life invigorated!

THE TIME AND PLACE FOR QUICKIES

𝒯he term "quickie" can have several different meanings. It can be quick sex for both when you are really pressed for time and you are both interested. Or a quickie can be a gift one gives to the other. There are some very stressful stages in parenting when having quickies is about all you can manage to do, but it keeps love alive for the time when

Love Life Enhancers

• Make appointments and write them on your love calendar.

• Choose time next week to experiment.

• Have a lunch date in a hotel (some hotels actually have cheap "date rates").

• Borrow a friend's house or condo for a half-day love date.

• Start your own Monday morning tradition.

• Set the alarm and get up thirty minutes earlier.

• Put kids to bed early and have a candlelight dinner for two.

• Bring home your children's favorite video.

• Plan a getaway (intensive sex school!).

you can enjoy longer, more satisfying sex. However, it is very important that neither partner feel used.

Sometimes intercourse is not possible or desirable. At such times you can stay sexually intimate by pleasuring each other. These times might include

• the last stages of pregnancy
• before resuming sexual intercourse after the birth of a baby
• when one mate is just too tired
• when one mate is sick or for some other reason doesn't want to have intercourse
• when a stress reliever is needed
• when you need to balance the differences in your sex drives

Eleven

~

The Fun Factor

"What did you mean, Claudia, when you said Dave was your best friend?" asked Holly during a Marriage Alive seminar break. "We've been husband and wife for nineteen years and have had five children together. We love each other and work together well, but I don't understand what you mean when you said we should be best friends."

"Holly, suppose you have a few spare minutes," Claudia responded. "You could use them to tidy up the kitchen, read a magazine, or spend time with your husband. If you choose to spend time with your husband over the other things, you are probably best friends."

WHO IS YOUR BEST FRIEND?

Do you consider your spouse your best friend? Do you look for ways to spend time together? Do you laugh together? Do you have fun with each other? All are symptoms of friendship and symptoms of a great marriage. Maybe you've been neglecting your friendship. The cares and concerns of parenting and providing for your family can be so overwhelming that you overlook having fun together. But in a healthy marriage and love life, having fun is serious business.

Can you think of one couple who has divorced who were still having fun with each other? We can't!

According to a recent survey, the amount of fun partners have together was the strongest factor in overall marital happiness. "Good relationships become great when you're preserving both the quantity and the quality of your fun times together."[1]

> **Friendship Enrichers**
>
> Take some couple time and develop a shared interest, activity, or sport. Consider the following:
>
> - Learn to line dance or square dance.
> - Reserve court time at a local tennis club.
> - Buy a subscription to a season of theater or opera.
> - Join a bridge club.
> - Take a cooking class together.
> - Start a dating club.

The next year Holly and her husband, Rick, attended another seminar with us. The first day Holly eagerly related the following story. "Remember last year when I asked you what you meant when you said you were each other's best friend? Well, now I know. This past year Rick and I have become best friends. I stopped being such a perfectionist and chose to spend more time with Rick. It worked! In our twenty years of marriage this last year has been the best—in spite of having teenagers in our home! We have taken the time to be friends and have fun together. It's even energized our love life and added freshness and romance to our relationship!"

We could tell by the sparkle in their eyes she was telling us the truth! If fun and friendship in marriage are so positive, why do we get married, have kids, and then take a vow of seriousness? What happened to the fun we had before we were married? Fun is one of the main reasons we got married; we enjoyed being together. "Time spent playing together provides a relaxed kind of intimacy that strengthens the bond between two people. So why does fun go by the wayside for many couples when it's such a large part of developing the relationship in the first place?" ask Drs. Markman, Stanley, and Blumberg.[2]

Fun times together set the tone for your whole family. Fun and laughter release tension, help build positive memories, and strengthen family relationships. Even to this day we have a cat puppet named Humor that we pull out at needed times. Perhaps you've heard the statement "The family that prays together stays together." We would add, "The family that laughs together lasts!"

If the "fun quotient" is low in your family, stop and ask why. Perhaps you take yourself too seriously. Or are you too busy to take the time for fun? Maybe you think fun is just for kids, or maybe it never even occurs to you to have fun. Just like working on your love life or developing any worthy habit, learning to have fun takes some commitment and certainly takes an investment of time. We hope you've already integrated some healthy habits into your lifestyle, like nurturing yourself and blocking out time for your love life. Now make sure that your couple times and family times are fun-filled. Here are some practical suggestions to increase your family's fun factor.

BECOME BEST FRIENDS

*B*ecome best friends with your mate. Best friends enjoy the same activities; they love to talk with each other; they love to joke around together. Fortunately, all these aspects of friendship can be nurtured if they are not already present.

Start a Dating Club

You can build a closer friendship while helping other couples do the same, by organizing your own dating club! Follow these simple six steps.

1. Find several other couples who want to develop more togetherness in their marriage. Think of like-minded friends—other couples at church, at work, in your parenting or couples' group.

2. Choose a date night. Once a week, every other week—even once a month could be really enriching!

3. Find regular child care. This may be the most daunting task, but it's not impossible. Consider challenging your church to offer free or low-cost child care once a month so couples in the church can fortify their marriages. If you belong to a parenting support group that provides child care during meetings, perhaps the child care workers would be willing to make themselves available for your date night. Get your individual sitter or consolidate kids at someone's home and bring in several trusted sitters. Keep brainstorming until you find something that works for you.

4. Pick a theme for each date. This will help you stay on target and will help you develop new common interests as a couple and as a couples' group. Choose a book or resource that offers themes for dates. (For instance, our new resource *10 Great Dates to Revitalize Your Marriage* [Zondervan, 1997] contains tear-out pages for ten dates with marriage-enriching themes. Short video date launches are also available.)

5. Take turns with the other couples in facilitating your fifteen- to twenty-minute date launch. Introduce the theme for the date and encourage couples to have fun!

6. Then have fun dating your mate! And remember to come back and pick up your kids!

Do Things Together

If you feel distance in your relationship—perhaps you are no longer able to just play together as you did before kids arrived—take some of the couple time you have set aside for each week and develop a shared interest, activity, or sport.

Remember, your kids will wait while you grab some time to build your friendship, but your marriage won't wait until your kids grow up!

Talk, Talk, Talk

If it seems you never have anything to talk about but the kids, it's time to take action. Select a book for both of

---

How Much Do You Know About Your Mate?
Play "Tell Me"!

Either one of you starts the game. Ask a question about yourself that the other must try to answer, such as, "Tell me how I would spend an evening if I could do anything I wanted."

The game's purpose is to deepen your knowledge of each other. The subjects may range from heavy ("Tell me my position on ecology") to light ("Tell me my favorite flavor of gum"). Here are some questions to get you started.

1. Tell me one subject I would like to study.
2. Tell me two comic strips I read regularly.
3. Tell me which place I would visit first in a strange city—the museum or the shopping mall.
4. Tell me the funniest person I know.
5. Tell me my favorite saying.
6. Tell me what color I think I look best in.

Once you get started, you may have trouble stopping. At least, you'll end the game with some new insights about your mate. Why not try it and find out for yourself?

Humor Helpers

- Buy a good joke book.
- Cut cartoons out of the paper and put them on your refrigerator.
- When you get up in the morning, do a silly dance.
- Choose a wild outfit to wear that will keep a smile on your face throughout the day.
- Feed your children something strange for breakfast (once Claudia served popcorn!).
- Tuck a bizarre note or toy into lunch boxes.
- Leave a joke on e-mail for your mate.
- Short sheet the bed.

you to read and then set aside an evening to discuss it. Choose a periodical or newspaper that you both will commit to read regularly and then pick one article for discussion each day at dinner. Conversation may be awkward at first, but as long as you encourage each other's expression of thoughts instead of tearing them down, you'll both eventually get good at the art of conversation.

How much do you really know about your mate? Most couples talk about everything except themselves, so you may be surprised to discover how much you don't know about your mate's personal likes and dislikes—no matter how long you've been married. To discover what your mate is thinking and to find out about his or her personal preferences, play the game "Tell me" (see p. 139).

Cultivate Humor

Even the most serious among us can find something funny every now and then. Think about what makes you laugh—a funny movie, a good joke, a bad joke, irony, crazy stunts—and intentionally seek these out. As you go through your day, think about funny situations in your home life or work life and relate them to the other members of your family. Your stories may seem a little dull at first, but you'll get better at telling them.

One of the best ways to cultivate humor is to let it happen. Often we are so concerned about offending someone or maintaining our composure that we stifle funny moments. So lighten up and let go when it comes to humor.

Psychologists tell us that a change in attitude can come about by a change in behavior. This means that if you take the first step of looking for humor and fun in your life and adding it in little ways even when you don't feel like it, your enjoyment of these activities will increase over time. Look for fun and add it to your life.

All of your antics might not be appreciated, but you will eventually find out what the other members of your family find funny, and you can fine-tune your funny bone in the process.

CELEBRATE FAMILY NIGHT

Just as you set aside one night each week for couple time, set aside one night for a special evening of family fun. The purpose of this evening is to do something fun as a family and build memories and relationships in the process. Just make sure that your events are planned, inclusive, and provide sufficient talking and joking time.

BENEFITS OF FUN

Whether the fun you have is as a couple or as a family, the benefits will flow to everyone. Keeping fun alive encourages family members to interact and stay in touch with what is going on in each other's lives. Laughter diffuses

Five Fun Family Nights

1. Rent a movie together, make popcorn, curl up on the sofa together, and then talk about the movie after it's over. Discuss: Who was your favorite character? What values did the story teach?

2. Have a game night with special snacks and prizes for the winner.

3. Cook a meal together. Homemade pizza is really easy, and even young children will enjoy playing with the dough and choosing toppings.

4. Get season tickets to see a professional sports team.

5. Make a family video production. Let your children videotape the two of you doing something silly, like dancing or snuggling on the couch.

Add to Your Family Fun

Fun times together set the tone for your whole family. Fun and laughter release tension, help build positive memories, and strengthen family relationships. Consider the following:

- Have a bear hunt. Hide all the stuffed toys throughout your home and let your children try to find them. While they are hunting, you can grab a few minutes to focus on each other.

- Take a family nature hike. Make a scavenger list and see who can find the most items on the list—a leaf, a dead bug, a small stone, and so on.

- Play family charades.

- Choose a family motto or design a family crest.

tension and helps you keep short accounts with one another. When your home is fun, children are generally happier and more content to let parents have some alone time. As a couple, you will be more focused on each other— and most important, this element of play can carry over to the bedroom!

In hopes of further facilitating the fun you have as a couple, we have stuffed the next two chapters full of practical suggestions and tips for creating special weekend getaways and crafting intimate mini-moments throughout each day.

Twelve

~

"Meet Me in Paris"

Arnold and Martha, parents of three children, survived fourteen years without a single twenty-four-hour period alone together. Arnold is a pastor, so weekends are his high-stress, heavy workload days. Weekend getaways weren't even a possibility—until he got creative.

Martha excitedly told us how Arnold called and made middle-of-the-week reservations for a lovely room with a view at the same hotel where they had spent their honeymoon years ago. He even reserved tables for each meal and arranged for someone to stay with their children. Martha was impressed! Here's what she told us: "I felt so loved. The thought of going was a gift as lovely as the actual getaway. Two whole days with no telephone calls, no figuring out which child needs to be where, no driving kids to soccer, no picking kids up from ballet, no preparing dinner for the whole gang or hassling over table manners—just time for Arnold and me! Actually, getting out of the routine was worth at least a week away on a desert island!"

~

Rebecca knew that her husband, Kyle, was under immense pressure at work. It had been ages since their last getaway,

Obstacle 1: The Budget Is Too Tight

Obstacle overcomers:

- Borrow someone else's home or condo.
- Clip coupons.
- Take food.
- Open a special "getaway account" and save.

so she decided to do something about it. Listen to her story: "Kyle had been so busy at work. We kept talking about getting off for a weekend, but it just wasn't happening. So I decided to take the initiative. The hardest part was finding baby-sitters for our two children. Our budget was tight, so I arranged for our two boys to stay with their cousins.

"Kyle's boss was fascinated with what I was doing, so he secretly arranged for Kyle to get off early on Friday. I baked Kyle's favorite chocolate chip cookies and packed the car. Then I drove to his office and kidnapped him! The getaway took time and effort to plan, but the look on Kyle's face when he realized what I was doing made it all worth it!"

Kyle agreed. "I never know what Rebecca is going to do next, but this time she really surprised me! On that Friday afternoon she just showed up at my work and pulled out a blindfold. Everyone in my office knew what was going on except me. The next thing I knew, I was in the car and she was telling me to relax, that she was kidnapping me for a getaway weekend.

"An hour and a half later the car stopped. She removed the blindfold and we were at our favorite mountain lodge in the Smoky Mountains. From

A Word to the Wise

If your spouse beats you to it and you find yourself being whisked away blindfolded to a romantic place, just relax, be cooperative, enjoy the process, and consider yourself extremely lucky.

there it just got better. I didn't think even once the entire time about all the pressure I was under at work!"

WHY GETAWAYS ARE NEEDED

*A*rnold and Martha and Rebecca and Kyle know firsthand that pulling off a getaway is a lot of work, but they told us it was well worth it. A focused time away gives you a chance to regroup, reignite romance, and deepen your marital bond. We are convinced that getaways aren't just fun to do, they are critical and necessary!

A getaway doesn't mean flying to the Bahamas or Europe for romance, it doesn't mean visiting the honeymoon suite at the best hotel in town, and it doesn't mean entertaining your spouse for every moment. A successful getaway is simply a chance for the two of you to be together, enjoy each other's company, and focus on loving each other. We do have two tips: go alone (not with your kids or with other couples), and before your getaway talk about your expectations.

Obstacle 2: The Children Are Too Young

Obstacle overcomers:

- It's for their own good!
- Kids are survivors.
- They won't go away!
- Others can care for your children.

GREAT EXPECTATIONS

*I*t only takes one of you to make the physical arrangements for your getaway, but both of you should talk about your expectations for the time away (unless you are kidnapping your mate). Sometimes we make a list of things

Obstacle 3: There's No One to Keep Our Children

Obstacle overcomers:

- Swap children with friends.
- Start a child care cooperative with other families.
- Save up and hire a sitter.
- Recruit relatives.
- Adopt grandparents, aunts, and uncles.

we are looking forward to. For instance, Dave usually looks forward to sleeping late and taking life easy. Claudia hopes to get in a long walk together and to start reading the mystery novel that has been collecting dust on her night table. We both look forward to making love.

Avoid overplanning your getaway. You want to come home relaxed, refreshed, and rested, not totally exhausted from an overstructured getaway. If you are more comfortable with some structure, our book *The Ultimate Marriage Builder* (a do-it-yourself getaway guide)[1] includes short exercises designed to improve your marriage and facilitate intimacy. We are also including a few suggestions and conversation starters in this chapter. But use them only if a little structure is appealing to you. As parents, the most important aspect of your weekend may be simply getting away without your kids, feeling like adults again, and concentrating on that part of your life most compromised by children—your love life.

GREAT GETAWAY PAYOFFS (WHY YOU'RE DOING THIS!)

*H*ere is what others are telling us about their getaways.

- "Our getaway was more fun than I expected. My favorite part of the weekend was watching an old movie and eating snacks while we were snuggled under the covers. My husband hates crumbs in the bed, so we never get to do that at home."

- "We loved holding hands, listening to music, and talking about our memories. We even wrote them down to save for posterity. We definitely plan to make getaways part of our future!"
- "Our weekend getaway was terrific! We spent a lot of time walking and talking. We even rented mopeds for Saturday afternoon—something we haven't done for years!"
- "We spent hours just talking. We relaxed, ate ice cream, bought T-shirts, and walked barefooted along the beach. We splashed with our feet in the cold water and decided we would take up sailing one day! When Sunday came, we didn't want to go home!"

PLAN YOUR GETAWAY

It's your turn to plan a getaway. Remember to make your agenda flexible, fun, and focused. Marriage is a marathon, not a sprint, and a getaway is not a onetime event. It's something you will want to repeat time and time again. You

---

Three Ss for a Successful Getaway

1. *Seclusion.* You need to get away from the paralyzing pressures of parenthood and the daily work routine and focus on each other. Leave computers and beepers at home.
2. *Stimulus.* Take along romantic music, a book of love poems, body lotion, your favorite classic romantic video (like *Casablanca*), or whatever puts you in a loving mood.
3. *Sex.* Getaways are a great time to explore and experiment. Take your favorite how-to book or take this book along.

Obstacle 4: There's No Time for a Getaway

Obstacle overcomers:

- Start with a twenty-four-hour getaway.
- Schedule one on next year's calendar.
- Put it on the top of your priority list.

---

don't want to feel as though you have an agenda you must follow. Instead relax. Have fun. Love each other. Just enjoying each other will bring new luster to your love relationship!

Plan Ahead for Romance

What conjures up romance in your mind? Candlelight, bubble bath, soft music? Make your own list and take along whatever you would like to have for romancing your mate. You may want to bring little gifts for each other. One wife gave her husband boxer shorts with hand-painted hearts all over them. Later he said real love was wearing those boxer shorts to work because they were the only clean pair he had! Of course, their children thought the boxer shorts were cool!

Getting There

If you are like most parents we know, plan to arrive somewhat exhausted. You may even wonder if the hassle of getting the children settled and getting to your destination is really worth it. Trust us, it is! You can relax and savor a

---

Getaway Box

Before your getaway, designate a getaway box. You can decorate it if you like. Put in the box anything you want to take on your getaway, such as candles and candleholders, matches, music cassettes or CDs with a player, your favorite snacks, drinks, your wedding pictures, your favorite devotional guide, your personal journal. As you pack your box, think about how much fun it is going to be to romance your mate.

quiet, romantic time alone. Your parenting job will be waiting for you when you arrive home after the get-away. For now entrust your children to the capable hands in which you left them, and for the next couple of days concentrate on each other.

Rekindling the Spark

Part of the secret of rekin-dling the old spark is to remember when the fires of love and romance were first lit. Think back to your dating days and when you first met. Remember and talk about your own unique story.

What's Next?

No pressure. No expectations. A romantic getaway is a time to simply enjoy the comfort of each other's company— to be lovers and to forget that you are parents. The guiding principle for a great getaway is that whatever you do should be desirable and pleasing for both.

You don't need props, but a filled getaway box can add a nice touch. However, if you are pressed for time and are just happy to be away, take advantage of your hotel's bathtub and provided toiletries. Be as creative as you can about finding interesting places or ways to make love. Remember, you don't have to pick up the mess, so don't worry about throwing the sheets and blankets off the bed or splashing water all over the bathroom floor.

Magic Moments

What do you remember about your

- first date
- first kiss
- favorite dates
- engagement
- wedding day
- honeymoon
- anniversaries
- romantic moments[2]

FAVORITE COUPLE GETAWAYS

Getaways will be as varied and unique as the couples who experience them. But to help you brainstorm, we're including some comments from couples who have successfully pulled off a romantic getaway.

Golfing in the Snow Getaway

"One January we hired a sitter to spend the weekend with our toddler and took off for an overnight getaway at a local park lodge. Our room overlooked a frozen lake and snow-covered golf course. On Saturday afternoon we played a round of winter golf. The whole golf course was ours. As we drove around the course in our golf cart, looking for our

---

Growing Deeper in Our Love and Commitment

Use these questions as conversation starters to help you evaluate your love life and think about where you want it to grow in the future.

- What are the positive factors about our love life?
- What changes do we need to make to keep it fresh and growing?
- At the present time what are our resources for nurturing our love life (things like health, faith in God, prayer, finances, time, adequate child care, and so on)?
- If someone looked at us, what would he or she say were our current priorities? Are they in the right order?
- What role does spiritual intimacy play in our relationship with each other?
- What is our most romantic fantasy? Could our fantasy become reality someday?
- What do we want our love life to look like in ten years? Twenty-five years?

orange golf balls in the snow, we talked continuously and with no interruptions!"

Romancing Your Mate Getaway

"On our getaway we experienced romance again! It is a marvelous, freeing experience, like reaching the summit of a mountain! And it was wonderful not to worry about our little interruptions—our three- and five-year-olds! I was able to relax and concentrate on loving my husband. We took perfumed candles and our portable CD player with our favorite Harry Connick Jr. and Stevie Wonder CDs."

A Timeless Getaway

"It's hard to get my wonderful, workaholic, time-oriented husband to agree to go off for a getaway. But once we get there, he relaxes and enjoys it almost as much as I do. One thing we really enjoy is sleeping late each morning. (Normally we live such structured, time-driven lives!) No travel alarm clocks allowed on our getaway! And we take off our watches and totally ignore the time. If we want to breakfast at 11:00 A.M. and lunch at 3:00 P.M., so what? Once we popped popcorn at 3:00 A.M. and fed it to each other in bed."

Obstacle 5: The Other Half Isn't Interested

Obstacle overcomers:

- Offer to do all the planning.
- Plan around something you know your spouse enjoys.
- Kidnap him or her.
- Ask for a getaway as a present.

Looking at the Future Getaway

"One of our most significant getaways was the time when we looked seriously at our love life and set some goals for the future. What worked so well for us was to write out our thoughts and desires. We both had time to reflect on our marriage and our love life and evaluate our goals and plans, without the kids interrupting and climbing in bed with us."

Romantic getaways can be the beginning of a new, improved love life. Focused times away can fan the fires of intimacy, passion, and commitment in your love relation-

Why Get Her Away?

Home may be your castle, but it may be your wife's "on location" job site. When our boys were young, the Arp house was best described as a zoo. At times Claudia, as the resident zookeeper and mama bear, desperately wanted and needed some release time. As the papa bear, to relax I wanted my easy chair, a Diet Coke, and a few minutes in my own little world.

I couldn't understand why Claudia didn't see home as a haven of rest and a great place for a "stay-at-home" getaway. Right or wrong, she simply felt more responsibility to keep the home fires burning—noses wiped, diapers changed, and meals on the table. At home, everywhere she looked there were things waiting to be done. In other words, from time to time home is a place you need to get away from! Finally it dawned on me that for most moms, relaxing at home was like dating at work.

Why not take the initiative? Plan a getaway for the two of you. Just think about what it will mean to your wife.

Whether she works outside the home or is a "stay-at-home" mom, she is a working mother! One mother who previously taught school but is now home with her preschoolers says it's actually more exhausting to be home with her three children than to teach a whole class of seventh graders! So whatever your situation, give the mother of your children a break. Plan an "out of the home" experience!

Dave

ship. They can help you hold on to your love in the midst of the hectic parenting years. Cherish your times away alone; fight for them. Be willing to do whatever it takes to keep planning love getaways—they are a great investment in your marriage. And you will pass on a legacy of love to your children!

Obstacle 6: There's No Energy

Obstacle overcomers:

- Go to a hotel room in your own town.
- Keep it simple. Eat out.
- Plan ahead.
- If you're too tired, you need it![3]

Thirteen

~

Marriage
Mini-Moments

*F*rom time to time we join our friends Kevin Lehman and Randy Carlson on their nationally syndicated radio program *Parent Talk*. Daily they look for ways to encourage parents. During one of our visits, we were talking with Kevin and Randy about our book *52 Dates for You and Your Mate*, and they asked listeners to call in and tell us how they romance their mates while parenting their children.

One mom called in with a great story: "Our tenth anniversary was coming up and our finances were really limited, so I went to a florist and asked for twelve long stems. (Without the roses, the stems were free!) Then I went to the grocery store and bought twelve Snickers bars—my husband's favorite candy. On each long stem I tied a candy bar with a red bow. Voilà! On our anniversary I presented him with a homemade card and a dozen long-stemmed Snickers bars. He'll always remember that anniversary!"

That's just one of the great ideas we've picked up from *Parent Talk*. Randy and Kevin are full of them—like "Sex begins in the kitchen." (That's also the title of one of Kevin's books.) He has five kids, so he must know! We do know that he and his wife, Sandy, have a great love relationship. So what does he mean by saying sex begins in the kitchen?

He emphasizes that sex begins wherever you are. It encompasses all that you are and all that you do. Sex is played out in a marriage within the context of the whole relationship. So picking up a dish towel in the kitchen and asking, "How was your day?" or turning off the TV in the living room and talking instead affects your love life. Does your attitude say, "I'm interested in you, I love you, and I look forward to our next time of intimacy and physical closeness?" You can answer yes if, in little acts and innuendoes, you express kindness throughout the day.

DISCOVER WHAT WORKS FOR YOU

*I*n a recent magazine article the writer shared how she collected tips for having a great sex life and tried them with her husband. Several were big bombs! A few worked. But her conclusion was that you need to find what works for you and what suits your personality.

We too have collected tips—from those who have participated in our seminars and surveys and from readers of our "You and Your Spouse" column in *Christian Parenting Today*. We have categorized the best mini-moment tips to make it easy for you to pick and choose from among them. Chuckle at the ones that are too far-out for your taste, and try the ones that feel good to you.

Time-Bound Moments
In the Morning

- Kiss good morning.
- Spend your first waking moments cuddling in bed with nondemand touching.

- Make a cup of tea or coffee for your spouse and bring it to him or her.
- Leave a message in the steam on the bathroom mirror. If you write it when you shower, it will reappear when your mate showers.
- Make your bed together.
- Take complete responsibility for the kids in the morning so your spouse can have extra time to sip coffee, read the paper, or get dressed.
- Bring in a flower from the garden—or even a dandelion—when you get the morning paper or take out the trash.

"Today I Love You Because ..."

"I went to an antique store and bought an old wooden recipe card box, took a wood burner, and burned in my wife's name and some flowers on top. Then on the front I added, 'Today I love you because ...'

"The first card in the box talked about the age and beauty of the wood, like our marriage. And it promised that there were far more reasons I love her than this box could ever hold. Every day since that day (three months ago), I have made a four-by-six card that starts with the words 'Today I love you because...' Some reasons are funny, some are serious.

"Before I leave the house every morning, I leave a card somewhere I know she will find it, like in the refrigerator, in her car or purse, or hidden in the morning paper. This exercise has had two very wonderful benefits. First, it forces me to think hard about why I really do love my wife today. Second, it may take a long time, but by golly, she's eventually going to believe me."

A creative husband

> ### "I Just Paged to Say 'Hello!'"
>
> "My husband and I both have pagers. When we're thinking of each other throughout the day but don't have time to talk on the phone, we page each other with 07734, which spells "hello" upside down. It makes me stop and smile to be reminded he's thinking about me."
>
> A creative wife

- Put toothpaste on your spouse's toothbrush while he or she is in the shower.
- Shower together.
- Kiss good-bye.
- Call your spouse on the cellular phone as he or she drives to work and wish him or her a good day.

At Work

- Clean out the car and leave a hot cup of coffee in a commuter mug for your spouse's trip to work.
- Make a tape of favorite love songs that your spouse can play in the car or at the office.
- Have pencils made with a special love message. Leave these in your spouse's pen holder.
- Make a mouse pad with a picture of the two of you. (These are available at most photo shops.)
- Send e-mail or voice mail messages of love.
- Meet for a romantic lunch.
- Send a care package with toiletries for the office.
- Use love codes on pagers or voice mail.
- Send flowers.
- Give your spouse a gift certificate for a service he or she can enjoy on a lunch hour: manicure, massage, shoe shine.

High-Stress Times

- Give your spouse a one-minute shoulder rub.
- Brush your spouse's hair.
- Relieve your mate of his or her usual duties so he or she can escape for a walk around the block.
- Order pizza.
- Make a joke.
- Give your spouse a hand or foot massage.
- Hug.
- Give your spouse a passionate kiss.
- Go to the neighbor's house and call your spouse with a special message of love.
- Kiss her hand.
- Write a quick note and slip it in his pocket.
- Smile.
- Hug and kiss until the kids find you.

> **Prayer Power**
>
> "Sneak time to pray together. This kept us going through five years of sheer terror raising kids."
>
> Survey participant

Evening Moments

- Change into something more comfortable.
- Light a candle.
- Draw her a bath.
- Fingerplay while doing dishes.
- Give away your television.
- Share your dessert together after the kids are occupied or in bed.

> **Snuggle Time for Two**
>
> "After we put the kids to bed at night, we take a few minutes and lie in bed and talk and snuggle."
>
> Survey participant

- Rent a romantic video.
- Give each other twenty minutes of private time after the kids are in bed.
- Snuggle while reading bedtime stories with the kids.

Creative Gift Giving

- Matching bathrobes
- Matching coffee cups
- A cellular phone for intimate conversations only
- A kite
- A book to share
- Cologne or perfume
- A filled Christmas stocking in July
- Season tickets to a sporting event, symphony, or theater
- Hiking boots
- Wildflowers
- A picnic basket for two
- A photo album
- An oil lantern

Ways to Say, "I Love You" (Notes, Notes, and More Notes)

- E-mail

A Trail of Love

"Once I was out on a Saturday afternoon, and when I returned, my husband had left a trail of notes that led to our bedroom. In the bedroom was romantic music, two glasses, a bottle of sparkling cider, and my husband. The boys were napping, so we enjoyed a romantic interlude!"

A satisfied wife

- Voice mail
- Singing telegrams
- Pager
- Audiotape
- Notes in drawers
- Notes in briefcases
- Written in steam on the mirror
- Written in catsup on a hot dog
- Written in a real love letter
- Mowed in the lawn
- Written on "love fortunes" baked into cookies (dough is available at Asian markets)

A Welcome-Home Surprise

"When one of us is out while the other is home with the kids, we leave notes on the door to surprise the one that's out of the house. One note said that a hot bath and back rub were waiting inside for me."

A creative husband

Sex-Specific Moments

- Get out the whipped cream.
- Develop an "I want you" code you can use in front of your children.
- Light candles and turn on soft music in your bedroom.

Let Your Marriage Bloom!

"Before we were married, I bought my husband a rosebush. He is more into gardening than I am. On each of the branches I put a little tag about cultivating our future love and marriage. I made him read each one before he planted the bush. Now our rosebush is a reminder of our love and how with tenderness, nourishment, and care it will grow into a beautiful flower."

A creative wife

- Drop flower petals along the path from the kitchen to the bedroom.
- Give your mate an intimate touch or kiss when the kids aren't looking.
- Offer to take over your spouse's evening chores while he or she takes a bath or otherwise prepares for loving.
- Pull down the covers on the bed and leave a candy mint on the pillow.

Fourteen

Loving for a Lifetime

The dinner was exquisite, the atmosphere romantic. The setting? A thirteenth-century castle set high on a hill overlooking the medieval town of Esslingen, Germany. Sharing the evening were our friends Helga and Hans. Between us we had logged over fifty-three years of marriage—more than some couples share in a lifetime. Thoughts of what marriage was like in the thirteenth century gave way to a conversation about what marriage is like today.

"What's happening to marriages here in Germany is disturbing," Hans told us. "Even before couples are married, most lack the commitment to love each other for a lifetime!" He went on to explain that often in the more modern marriage ceremony liturgy, couples no longer promise to stay together "until death do us part." Instead they promise to stay married "until our love dies." No wonder so many marriages in Germany don't last for a lifetime.

And for those couples who remain married for a lifetime (in Germany and in the United States), how many have unreported premature deaths of their love life? Love and intimacy in a marriage grows by stages, but if we ignore our sexual relationship at any stage, it can shut down and die. How can we keep the flame of love burning through all the years ahead? Happy Honey in Honolulu has some advice. She wrote the following letter to "Dear Abby."

Dear Abby,

> Your reader thinks most women "fake it." Well, here's one who doesn't have to. Even though my husband is seventy-nine and I'm seventy-six, sex is still fun. We love to have our children visit us for a day or two, but when they leave, I put the red satin sheets on the waterbed, turn on some soft music, and don my sexiest nightie. Then, let the fun begin. Believe me, faking isn't necessary.
>
> Happy Honey in Honolulu[1]

Red satin sheets and waterbeds may not be your style, but if you build your marriage and keep your love life alive through all the stages of your marriage, you may still be enjoying each other in your seventies, like Happy Honey— and perhaps in your eighties as well.

Now is the time to decide what you want your love life to look like in your golden years. Stephen Covey, in his best-selling book *The Seven Habits of Highly Effective People,* writes about beginning with the end in mind. Take a few moments and reflect on what you want your love life and your marriage to look like when you have been married for forty or fifty years. Then compare your dreams for the future with the reality of today. This may help you identify the challenges ahead of you.

BUT YOU DON'T KNOW MY SPOUSE

I'm the one that is committed to my marriage," one friend told us. "I'm the one who wants a love life. I can't say the same thing about my husband. I don't think he could ever be romantic, and I don't know if he even cares."

Maybe you identify with our friend. You know that marriage includes living with someone who is less than perfect. We hate to admit it, but we still let each other down. We are continually challenged to forgive and accept each other. In our marriage, forgiveness is the oil that lubricates our love relationship.

It's hard if not impossible to make love to someone who is unaccepting or harboring a grudge. But forgiveness and acceptance can begin with one heart. If we choose to forgive our spouse, accept his or her negative qualities, and concentrate on his or her positive attributes, we give our spouse the freedom to grow and change.

One wife shared with us how she came to understand this principle: "I've been married for eleven years and have a seven-year-old and two preschoolers. Is our marriage healthy? I guess I'd say yes. Is it romantic, thriving, and growing? I'd probably say not really. Recently I've had to come to grips with the fact that my husband is not the romantic, sweep-me-off-my feet, answer-to-all-my-problems Prince Charming. Neither is he an abusive, alcoholic, workaholic maniac. He is a quiet, hardworking, unassuming, even-keeled man taking care of his responsibilities day by day.

"I'm more of the idealistic, romantic dreamer. In the past, whenever I had the chance, I would give my husband articles and books about 'putting romance in your marriage.' He'd try a few ideas, find it awkward, and drop it. Then I would become very discouraged. He seemed so ho-hum, so quiet. He's not the outgoing, gregarious type; he's more quiet and subdued. I began to realize I was asking him to be something he's not, nor ever has been, and probably will never be.

"During our courtship I was the note writer, the gift sender, the surprise planner. And at that time I didn't seem to mind his lack of romanticism. In fact, I was attracted to his solid, no-nonsense, logical, realistic grip on life. It balanced my own up-and-down moodiness and emotional view of life. Why is it that the very thing I was attracted to during courtship has become so irritating?

"I found that I was dwelling on the negatives and degrading him in my mind to such a point that I was unhappy in our marriage. I'm trying now to accept him as he is and look for the strengths and not the weaknesses. Sundays he's not up front as the dynamic leader—he's sitting next to me in the pew, looking at books with our four-year-old. He's not out leading a couples' or men's neighborhood study or leading the local Boy Scout troop—he's in the backyard, assembling a swing set. He's not the head of a company, earning lots of money—he's home every night at six to eat with us and bathe the kids to give me a break. He'll never be romantic like a Robert Redford or Tom Cruise, but he is loving in his own quiet way.

"It has been a process, but I have come to grips with who my husband really is versus my romantic expectations. I have learned that sometimes you have to accept and deal with your own shortcomings and not complain or envy others who seem to be in more 'ideal' situations. I need to keep doing what I can do, and that's my contribution to our love life and marriage."

Do you see yourself in this woman's comments? Perhaps revitalizing your marriage and love life depends on starting with you instead of your spouse. It takes one person's positive attitude and action to begin to move forward. Baby steps taken in good faith can make a tremendous difference. Why not pause right now and make a list of all the positive traits you see in your spouse? If there is something you need to forgive or ask forgiveness for, do it now. Then commit yourself to do all within your power to build a loving relationship with your spouse that will last for a lifetime.

CHERISH YOUR MARRIAGE AND CELEBRATE!

*C*herishing" means holding dear, nurturing, and celebrating. It is a natural outgrowth of a healthy relationship, but it can be developed on its own. Practically, cherishing your marriage includes verbalizing your love and commitment to your spouse and demonstrating that love in little, meaningful ways throughout your lifetime—and in big, spectacular ways every now and then. It means encouraging each other and affirming your relationship in private and in public. And it means celebrating your love for each other.

As we come to the close of this book, we think about our own marriage, as we have so often throughout the writing of this book. We hope we have given you a glimpse of a marriage that isn't perfect—one that is still at times very needy—but one in which together we continue to cherish and celebrate our love for each other. Having just celebrated our thirty-fifth anniversary, we have an extended marriage history. We have logged years and years as lovers and parents.

Within the walls of our home it is now quiet. Yet in the recesses of our mind we hear the echoes of happy children and treasure memories of the hectic parenting years when once we struggled to make time to build our love life while we raised our three sons. Now our sons are grown and married and have families of their own. We have passed on the baton of active parenting and the challenging task of building a love life while parenting kids.

And every now and then we once again hear little voices in our home, when our precious grandkids come to visit and fill our empty nest with the wonderful sounds of childhood. We see again the stresses, strains, and joys of parenting through the bloodshot eyes of our own children. Our wish for them and for you is to seize the day—in the middle of your hectic lives as you parent your kids, make time for loving each other.

Time for sex? Time for loving? Time for enjoying your marriage while you parent your children? It's there if you're willing to seize the day and make time for sex! It's there if you're willing to search for it. Only the wise will find it!

Postscript —

Habits of Highly Satisfied Lovers

~

As we conducted our national survey on love, sex, marriage, and kids, we had the opportunity to encounter so many couples who against incredible odds are finding creative ways to love each other and build successful love lives in the middle of family life. From our survey participants we learned a great deal about how to build a love life while parenting children. It is with great joy that we have passed on to you many of the wonderful suggestions and ideas we received from those creative lovers.

As we tabulated our survey, we observed several "habits" of couples who have built a highly successful love life, and we would like to wrap up this book with a list of some of those habits. Our hope is that we are describing you!

- They have an intentional marriage. They make time to dream and plan together.
- They have developed the habit of dating.
- They take regular getaways without their children.
- They give each other the freedom to grow and change.
- They practice the habits of forgiveness and acceptance.

Benefits of Building a Creative Love Life

- A creative love life will help "affair-proof" your marriage.
- You will stay emotionally connected.
- You will be better able to handle stress.
- Sex is good for your health.
- You will be a good role model for your children.
- You will have a future love life after the kids leave home and you do have time!

- They concentrate on the positive and build each other up.
- They love their children, are good parents, but give equal emphasis to their own relationship.
- They have a sense of humor.
- They are best friends and have fun together.
- They continue to read, attend seminars, and educate themselves about how to be better mates and lovers.
- They make time for sex!

Notes

Chapter Two — What's a Love Life?

1. Proverbs 24:26.
2. Proverbs 5:18–19.
3. Judith Wallerstein and Sandra Blakeslee, *The Good Marriage* (Boston, New York: Houghton Mifflin, 1995), 192.

Chapter Three — Revive Us Again

1. Paul Pearsall, *Super Marital Sex* (New York: Ivy, 1987), 28–29.
2. Ellen Kreidman, *Is There Sex After Kids?* (New York: St. Martin's Paperbacks, 1993), 79–80.
3. Proverbs 23:7 (New King James Version).
4. John Bradshaw, *Bradshaw on: The Family* (Deerfield Beach, Florida: Health Communications, 1988), 32.
5. Ibid.

Chapter Four — Building Blocks for Great Sex

1. David and Vera Mace, *Close Companions* (New York: Continuum, 1982), 96.
2. David Mace, *Love and Anger in Marriage* (Grand Rapids: Zondervan, 1982). This book may be ordered from the Association of Couples in Marriage Enrichment (A.C.M.E.), P.O. Box 10596, Winston-Salem, NC 27108 or call 1-800-634-8325.

We are grateful to David and Vera Mace for their input into our lives and marriage and for the excellent training we received from A.C.M.E. training workshops. Our basic philosophy of how to deal with anger and conflict is adapted from our training with the Maces and used with their permission. A.C.M.E. offers excellent leadership training for those interested in leading marriage enrichment groups.

Howard Markman, Scott Stanley, and Susan Blumberg, *Fighting for Your Marriage* (San Francisco: Jossey-Bass, 1994).

Drs. Markman, Stanley, and Blumberg are marital researchers and founders of the Prevention and Relationship Enhancement Program (PREP). PREP is a research-based approach to teaching couples how to communicate effectively, work as a team to solve problems, manage conflicts without damaging closeness, and preserve and enhance commitment and friendship. The PREP approach is based on twenty years of research in the field of marital health and success, with much of the research conducted at the University of Denver over the past fifteen years. For more information about PREP, write to PREP, Inc., P.O. Box 102530, Denver, CO 80250 or call (303) 759-9931.

3. John Gottman, Ph.D., *Why Marriages Succeed or Fail* (New York: Simon & Schuster, 1994), 29.

4. Pearsall, *Super Marital Sex* (New York: Ivy, 1987), 217.

5. "Making Sex a Spiritual Experience," *Lexington Herald-Leader* (February 15, 1997), 10 in "Today" section.

6. "Marriage in America," Council on Families in America, © 1995, Institute for American Values, 7.

Chapter Six — Love à la Carte

1. Clifford and Joyce Penner, *52 Ways to Have Fun, Fantastic Sex* (Nashville: Nelson, 1994), 73.

2. Robert and Rosemary Barnes, *Great Sexpectations* (Grand Rapids: Zondervan, 1996), 181.

3. Song of Songs 2:4 (New American Standard Bible).

Chapter Seven — No Time for Sex

1. Edwin Kiester Jr. and Sally Valente Kiester, "Sex After Thirty-five—Why It's Different, Why It Can Be Better," *Reader's Digest* (November 1995), 14.

2. Pearsall, *Super Marital Sex,* 16.

Chapter Eight — No Energy for Sex

1. Adapted from Jean Lush with Pamela Vredevelt, *Mothers and Sons* (Old Tappan, N.J.: Revell, 1988). Used by permission.

Chapter Nine — "Mommy and Daddy Are Busy Now"

1. Jan Dravecky with Connie Neal, *A Joy I'd Never Known* (Grand Rapids: Zondervan, 1996), 201–2.
2. Robert and Rosemary Barnes, *Great Sexpectations* (Grand Rapids: Zondervan, 1996), 108.

Chapter Ten — Sex on a Schedule

1. "Idea of a Perfect Evening," *Ladies Home Journal* (November 1994), 52.
2. Katy Koontz, "Is There Sex After Children?" *Reader's Digest* (February 1997), 34–35.

Chapter Eleven — The Fun Factor

1. Markman et al., *Fighting for Your Marriage*, 250.
2. Ibid.

Chapter Twelve — "Meet Me in Paris"

1. David and Claudia Arp, *The Ultimate Marriage Builder* (Nashville: Nelson, 1994).
2. Adapted from David and Claudia Arp, *10 Great Dates to Revitalize Your Marriage* (Grand Rapids: Zondervan, 1997).
3. Adapted from David and Claudia Arp, *Where the Wild Strawberries Grow* (Colorado Springs: Chariot/Victor, 1996).

Chapter Fourteen — Loving for a Lifetime

1. "Dear Abby," *Knoxville News-Sentinel* (September 16, 1991).

Ten Fun-Filled Couples' Nights Out® That Will Energize Your Marriage!

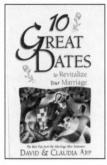

10 Great Dates to Revitalize Your Marriage
David & Claudia Arp
Softcover 0-310-21091-7

Dating doesn't have to be only a memory or just another boring evening at the movies. David and Claudia Arp have revolutionized dating by creating Couples' Nights Out®— memory-making evenings built on key, marriage-enriching themes. This approach to relationship growth involves both partners, is low-key, and best of all, is exciting, proven, and FUN!

Draw upon the best tips from David and Claudia Arp's popular Marriage Alive Seminars in this book, *10 Great Dates*. You'll learn how to:

- Communicate better
- Build a creative sex life
- Process anger and resolve conflicts
- Develop spiritual intimacy
- Balance busy lifestyles
- And more!

Also look for . . .
10 Great Dates to Revitalize Your Marriage Video Curriculum
ISBN 0-310-21350-9

This video curriculum is based on the Marriage Alive Seminars and the *10 Great Dates to Revitalize Your Marriage* book.

The curriculum kit contains:
- two 75-minute videos with ten short date launches
- one *10 Great Dates to Revitalize Your Marriage* softcover (204 pages)
- one Leader's Guide (48 pages)